# CORROSION OF BUILDING MATERIALS

# CORROSION OF BUILDING MATERIALS

**Dietbert Knöfel**
Professor, Gesamthochschule
Siegen, West Germany

Translated from the German by
**R.M.E. Diamant, M.Sc., Dip. Chem. E.,
M. Inst. F., C. Eng.**
University of Salford, England

 **VAN NOSTRAND REINHOLD COMPANY**
NEW YORK    CINCINNATI    ATLANTA    DALLAS    SAN FRANCISCO
LONDON    TORONTO    MELBOURNE

This book was originally published in Germany under the title Stichwort: Baustoffkorrosion
by Bauverlag GmbH copyright © 1975 by Bauverlag GmbH, Weisbaden and Berlin
Translation by R. M. E. Diamant
Library of Congress Catalog Card Number 77-27403
ISBN 0-442-23090-7

Printed in the United States.
Published in 1978 by Van Nostrand Reinhold Company
A division of Litton Educational Publishing, Inc.
450 West 33rd Street, New York, NY 10001

Van Nostrand Reinhold Limited
1410 Birchmount Road, Scarborough, Ontario M1P 2E7, Canada

Van Nostrand Reinhold Australia Pty. Limited
17 Queen Street, Mitcham, Victoria 3132, Australia

Van Nostrand Reinhold Company Limited
Molly Millars Lane, Wokingham, Berkshire, England

16   15   14   13   12   11   10   9   8   7   6   5   4   3   2   1

**Library of Congress Cataloging in Publication Data**

Knöfel, Dietbert.
  Corrosion of building materials.

  Translation of Stichwort Baustoffkorrosion.
  Bibliography: p.
  Includes index.
  1. Building materials—Corrosion. I. Title.
TA418.74.K5613      620.1′1223      77-27403
ISBN 0-442-23090-7

# PREFACE

Corrosion of building materials is nothing very new. Building sections have always been liable to destruction when exposed to corrosive groundwater or when wrongly used.

In recent years the problem has become more acute because of the increasing pollution of our environment. There is an increased outpouring of flue gases and effluents, and construction is now taking place on sites which have been purposely avoided in the past. The increasing shortage of raw materials, particularly of nonferrous metals, and their rising costs underline the importance of preventing corrosion damage in buildings.

The single most important factor in avoiding corrosion is knowledge why it is taking place. In this book the various corrosion processes and the preventive techniques are arranged according to the materials involved, in order of importance.

Building technologists should be able to carry out simple chemical tests themselves and must be capable of evaluating the results of more complex investigations; therefore, the last chapter outlines techniques of analysis.

This short book, which is intended only as a general introduction to the subject, is intended for practitioners and students of construction, to help them to understand and to avoid corrosion problems. The author would be grateful for suggestions as to how this book may be improved.

# CONTENTS

# CORROSION OF BUILDING MATERIALS

# 1
# INTRODUCTION

Corrosion is defined as the involuntary destruction of substances such as metals and mineral building materials by surrounding media, which are usually liquid (corrosive agents). It usually begins at the surface and is caused by chemical and, in the case of metals, electrochemical reactions. The destruction can then spread to the interior of the material. Living organisms may also contribute to the corrosion of building materials.

The economic importance of corrosion and corrosion protection can be shown by the following example: It is estimated that roughly 3% of the annual production of steel is lost by corrosion. In 1974, 140 million tons of steel were produced in the United States at a cost of approximately $400 per ton. This gives a monetary loss by corrosion of about 1.7 billion dollars. It is clearly of the utmost importance to reduce as far as possible the financial loss by corrosion, which not only affects steel but to some extent all other building materials as well.

The most common forms of metallic corrosion are caused by electrochemical reactions, wherein two metallic phases (e.g., iron oxide and iron) react in the presence of electrolytic solutions.

When concrete corrodes, the corrosive substances are carried to the building material by means of aqueous solutions (natural and industrial waters, gases dissolved in moisture, etc.). New, readily soluble compounds can be formed on the surface and cause solution corrosion. Swelling corrosion can take place by the formation of voluminous new compounds produced inside the material. In the case of building glasses and ceramic building materials, as with all mineral building materials, corrosion which depends only on purely chemical reactions is usually very slight.

**Table 1.1. Summary of the Most Important Forms of Corrosion Which Affect Building Materials.**

| Building material | Corrosive medium | Principal reaction |
|---|---|---|
| Metallic building materials | Electrolytic solutions[1] (At least two metallic phases are present) | Electrochemical reaction. The less noble metallic phase is removed. |
| | Salt solutions, acid or basic solutions such as natural and industrial waters | Chemical reaction which dissolves the material |
| Nonmetallic inorganic building materials | Salt solutions, acid or basic solutions such as natural and industrial waters | Chemical reaction which dissolves or swells the material |
| Organic building materials | Salt solutions, acid or basic solutions such as natural and industrial waters | Chemical reaction which dissolves, expands or embrittles the material |

[1]Electrolytic solutions are all solutions which contain ions, e.g., acids, bases, and natural and industrial waters.

Organic substances, particularly bituminous building materials and plastics, which are used for the protection of buildings, usually show excellent resistance against atmospheric attack.

Table 1.1 gives a general summary of the most important forms of corrosion of building materials.

The factors which cause the destructive reactions affecting building materials are manifold. The following are the most important:

*Physical factors:*
 Heat
 Temperature changes
 Frost
 Running water
 Solar radiation (particularly ultraviolet)
 Wind
 Dust

*Chemical factors:*
 Acids
 Alkalis
 Salt solutions
 Organic materials
 Flue gases

*Biological factors:*
  Microorganisms
  Fungi
  Algae
  Marine animals
  Worms
  Insects
  Multicellular plants

These factors may act singly, but usually they act in concert, and in this way the degree of corrosion is increased. The most important factors causing corrosion of building materials are generally chemical ones. In addition, humidity in its various forms (rain, condensation, fog, high atmospheric humidity, ground water, steam, ground humidity, bog water, seawater, lake water, and river water) is always a necessary precondition for corrosion under normal building conditions.

Different building materials are affected in very different ways by various aggressive media, or they may not be affected at all. Ultraviolet radiation causes the ageing of plastics but has no effect on metals or concrete. Even weak acids attack concrete and many metals, but only very few plastics. Organic solvents, like carbon tetrachloride, dissolve bituminous building materials but have no influence on mineral building materials. Certain microorganisms aid the corrosion of iron in soil, while fungi cause the destruction of timber. Many other examples could be cited.

Depending on the conditions encountered in connection with a specific building material at a specific site (climate, whether the material is above or below ground, etc.), one has to deal with a variety of different aggressive materials. Even within a certain range of specific uses, the nature of the corrosive agents may vary considerably. It is, for example, a matter of some importance whether galvanized steel sheeting is used in country air (clean air), city air, industrial air (badly polluted air) or sea air (containing salts). Industrial air and city air contain flue gases, which in their turn include sulfur dioxide ($SO_2$). This forms sulfurous acid ($H_2SO_3$) in the presence of moisture and, after oxidation, sulfuric acid ($H_2SO_4$). These acids attack not only zinc but also iron, concrete, etc. These matters will be dealt with more fully in the chapters which follow.

Quite apart from corrosion, purely mechanical processes may affect the surfaces of building materials and damage them. Flowing liquids which contain solid particles are an example; they cause erosion. If eroding media are chemically active at the same time, combined destruction may take place; this is called erosion–corrosion.

# 2
# CORROSION AND
# CORROSION PROTECTION
# OF HYDRAULIC MORTAR
# AND CONCRETE

## 2.1 FUNDAMENTALS

The destructive attack by materials which come into external contact with the concrete is the main cause for its corrosion. Destructive reactions which may be caused by concrete components such as water, cement, and ballast are not, strictly speaking, part of "concrete corrosion."

As far as mixing water is concerned, it should only be mentioned that most naturally occurring waters are suited for this purpose. As the chemical reactions with various compounds which may be present in the water take place before the cement sets, one would not expect any destruction from this quarter. On the other hand, there may be some interference with the setting process. A salt content of less than 3.5% by weight is in general not harmful, and even seawater can be used. Badly polluted waters, bog waters, and industrial effluents, which may contain carbohydrates or other organic materials, should be avoided. The rust protection of the reinforcement must not be endangered, and for this reason it is important that the chloride content should not be excessive. With prestressed concrete, $Cl^-$ must be less than 300 mg/liter. It is always best to use pure water (drinking water).

It is extremely unlikely that the cement itself would give any trouble because of the very thorough production control which is practised in cement works. Chalk, magnesia, and sulfate damage (caused by cement) are virtually unknown today. Ballast which corresponds to DIN 4226 or equivalent American specifications should also be completely satisfactory (section 2.3). The only form of corrosion with which we are concerned here is that of set concrete by external media.

Chemical attack on concrete and mortar is usually effected by water or aqueous solutions. Certain gases and soils too can have a destructive effect, but only when they are damp. According to recent research by the German engineers Sprung and Rechenburg, the age of the concrete has no effect on its liability to corrosion.

Detection of corrosive media at a site is often a matter of experience; but certain phenomena are clear warnings (see Table 2.1). Neighboring building sections which have been exposed to the same environmental conditions for appreciable periods of time provide further evidence. A geological or soil type map can be examined for evidence of the presence of sulfate rocks in the subsoil, and this will suggest a danger of concrete corrosion. Many industrial plants (e.g., breweries; tanneries; gasworks; dyeworks; mines; dairies; factories making preserves, soap, alkali, or sugar; glass etching plants; paint factories; bleachworks) also produce materials which damage concrete.

It is generally impossible to assess just by looking whether the local water will attack concrete. It is therefore advisable always, or at least when there is the slightest ground for suspicion, to carry out a water analysis. A preliminary simple water analysis can be carried out easily

Table 2.1.  Media Suspected of Causing Damage to Concrete.

| Waters | Soils | Gases |
| --- | --- | --- |
| Dark coloration | Soils with unusual color | Industrial flue gases |
| Obnoxious odor | Soils colored black to gray, particularly if they have reddish brown patches | Flue gases from coal fired or oil fired furnaces |
| Ascending gas bubbles | Soils which are bleached light gray to white underneath black humus soil | Gases which contain $H_2S$ on top of effluents |
| Salts separated out of solution | | |

with a Merck Aquaquant® kit.* With the kit, provided an adequate sampling technique is used, one can safely differentiate between corrosive and noncorrosive waters. If such a preliminary test indicates the presence of substances likely to attack concrete, the help of an established laboratory should be sought. The same applies if it is not possible to obtain a water sample analysis when there is indication that the soil is suspect.

To obtain reliable analysis figures and a correct assessment of the degree of attack to be expected, it is necessary to use an exact and representative sampling technique. For example, the water must not be diluted by rainwater and the various horizons of goundwater must not be mixed. Further details regarding methods of water analysis are to be found in chapter 8.

Concrete consists of cement and ballast, often with steel reinforcements. The ballast is usually stable against the aggressive media which arise. Exceptions are limestone and some other ballasts, which are dissolved by acid water, as well as ballast containing sheets of mica, in which gypsum can crystallize in the presence of sulfates and crack the concrete structure by swelling.

The cement is the part of the concrete which is most easily attacked. It is produced from the Portland cement clinker phase by reactions with water. The main components are:

tricalcium silicate, $C_3S$
dicalcium silicate, $C_2S$
tricalcium aluminate, $C_3A$
calcium aluminate ferrate, $C_2(A,F)$
gypsum, $Cs \cdot 2H$

These formulations use the cement notation. $C = CaO$, $S = SiO_2$, $A = Al_2O_3$, $F = Fe_2O_3$, $Cs = CaSO_4$, $H = H_2O$.

Depending upon the various initial phases, the new structures also differ very considerably from each other. A typical reaction is that of $C_3S$, which forms more than 50% by weight of Portland cement. It illustrates the complicated nature of the hydration of cement:

---

*Aquaquant® kits are presently unavailable in the United States. However, E. Merck is investigating the feasibility of marketing them in this country.

$$2(3CaO \cdot SiO_2) + 6H_2O \longrightarrow 3CaO \cdot 2SiO_2 \cdot 3H_2O + 3Ca(OH)_2$$

or

$$2C_3S + 6H \longrightarrow C_3S_2H_3 + 3CH$$

tricalcium silicate + water $\longrightarrow$ hydrated calcium silicate
+ calicum hydroxide

The set cement consists mainly of hydrated calcium silicate, calcium hydroxide, and reaction products originating from calcium aluminate (e.g., hydrated tetracalcium aluminate) and calcium aluminate ferrate. Hydrated calcium silicate, in particular, gives strength to concrete, while the calcium hydroxide is the reason for the alkaline nature of the set cement ($pH > 12$) and with it the final concrete.*

The products of hydration vary in their behavior against different aggressive media. Figure 2.1. shows the harmful effects upon concrete of these media.

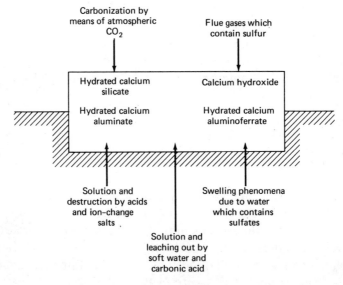

**Figure 2.1.** Destructive effects on concrete.

*The $pH$ value is a measure of the strength of acids and alkalis within the range $0-14$. The number corresponds to $-\log_{10}$ of the hydrogen ion concentration in moles per liter ($pH\ 7$ = neutral; $pH > 7$ = alkaline; $pH < 7$ = acid).

If water soluble reaction products are produced during the corrosive actions the set cement is dissolved from the surface: this is a *dissolving attack*. Among media causing dissolving attack are the following: acids, salts with exchangeable ions, soft water, organic oils, and fats.

If reaction products which are sparingly soluble and voluminous are produced inside the set cement during corrosion reactions, these expanding structures can exert pressure upon their surroundings, loosening the framework of the concrete. This is called a *swelling attack*. Swelling attacks are caused by sulfates, magnesium ions, and amorphous silicon dioxide.

Figure 2.2 shows both dissolving and swelling attacks. Both types of attack can occur simultaneously.

Complete hydration of cement theoretically requires about 30% water, i.e., a water to cement ratio of 0.3. After hardening, the excess water stays in the capillary pores of the concrete as a solution of calcium hydroxide. The more excess unbound water, i.e., the greater the water to cement ratio in excess of 0.3, the more porous the set concrete. The inner surface which can be attacked has a larger area, and corrosive solutions and gases can penetrate into concrete more easily.

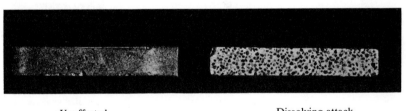

Unaffected                          Dissolving attack

Swelling attack

**Figure 2.2.** Swelling and dissolving attacks.

The reinforcement in reinforced and prestressed concretes is normally passivated by the presence of calcium hydroxide ($pH > 12$). It therefore cannot rust. The passivity of the reinforcement can be destroyed, however, by external agents. For example, $CO_2$ may be absorbed, and the resulting carbonation of the concrete may allow corrosion of the reinforcement; the strength of the steel is thereby reduced and the concrete which surrounds the steel can flake off. This will be described in detail in section 2.4.2.

## 2.2  CORROSION AND CORROSION PROTECTION OF SET CONCRETE

Table 2.2 gives a summary of the way various chemicals act upon set cement.

### Table 2.2.  Action of Certain Materials on Set Concrete.

| Material | Occurrence | Action |
|---|---|---|
| Fairly chemically pure water | Water of condensation, rainwater, molten snow, soft spring water. | Dissolves, leaches out. Active, in practice, when hardness is less than 1.1 milliequivalents |
| Inorganic acids (HCl, $H_2SO_4$, $H_2SO_3$, $HNO_3$, $H_3PO_4$, $H_2SiO_4$, $H_2CO_3$) | In the chemical industry, particularly carbonic and sulfurous acids. Also in natural waters. | Dissolves; the stronger the acid the more intensely corrosive it is. Increasing activity is also found with falling $pH$ value. Sulfuric acid has also a swelling effect. Carbonic acid corrosion depends upon free $CO_2$. |
| Organic acids Acetic acid, lactic acid, tannic acid, formic acid. | During fermentation in dairies, canneries, fodder silos, dyeworks, etc. | Dissolves slowly; can slow down setting process. |
| Humic acid | In soils and impure ballast. | Can attack slowly, depending upon type of humic acid. |
| Oxalic acid | Dyeworks, chemical factories. | Nondestructive. |
| Alkalis (sodium and potassium hydroxides) | In the chemical industry. | Dissolves only when highly concentrated. |

| | | |
|---|---|---|
| Plant and animal oils and fats (olive oil, rape seed oil, linseed oil, poppy seed oil, soya bean oil, fish oils, suet, shortening, lard) | Food industry and food trade. | Loosens the structure; dissolves by reaction of the fatty acids with calcium salts to form soft calcium soaps. Turpentine has no destructive effect. |
| Mineral oils and coal tar distillates (light oils, heavy oils, benzene, anthracene, paraffin, bitumen) | Engineering sheds, filling stations; refineries. | As these materials are non-acidic they are nondestructive. All low viscosity oils penetrate concrete and act as lubricants between set cement and ballast, to loosen structure. Phenol and cresol slowly corrode concrete. |
| Aqueous solutions | | |
| $Mg^{2+}$ | In natural and industrial waters. | Softens. |
| $NH_4^+$ | Agricultural undertakings, artificial fertilizer factories. | Dissolves. |
| $SO_4^{2-}$ | In natural and industrial waters. | Swells. |
| $pH$ less than 6.5 (acid) | In natural and industrial waters. | Dissolves. |
| carbon dioxide and carbonic acid | In natural waters, particularly if soft. | Dissolves. |
| $Na^+$, $K^+$, $Ca^{2+}$, $Fe^{2+}$, $Fe^{3+}$, $Al^{3+}$, $Si^{4+}$, $NO_3^-$, $PO_4^{3-}$, and $SiO_3^{2-}$ | In natural and industrial waters. | Not harmful. |

## 2.2.1  Attack by Solvent Action

*Attack by acids*

The degree of attack by acids depends upon their strengths and their concentrations. Strong mineral acids such as hydrochloric acid, sulfuric acid, and nitric acid dissolve *all* components of set cement, with the formation of calcium, aluminum and iron salts as well as silica gel.* Weak acids such as carbonic acid, and many organic acids such as humic acid and lactic acid, only form water soluble salts with some

*A typical reaction is the following:

$3CaO \cdot 2SiO_2 \cdot 3H_2O + 6HCl \longrightarrow 3CaCl_2 + 2SiO_2 + 6H_2O$

Hydrated calcium silicate + hydrochloric acid $\longrightarrow$

calcium chloride + silica gel + water (easily soluble)

calcium compounds. Severe damage is only to be expected after long periods of exposure.

Hydrogen sulfide ($H_2S$, smell of rotten eggs) is formed during the decomposition of organic materials, as in effluents. When it dissolves in water it forms a weak acid. It can be absorbed above the water level by the humidity of the concrete in effluent concrete pipes and then oxidized to form sulfurous and sulfuric acids. In both cases an acidic attack is mainly involved.

$SO_2$ gas, which is present in flue gases, can be converted in the presence of moisture into sulfurous acid and by oxidation into sulfuric acid. In this case the attack is also mainly an acidic one.

Strong acids may be present in effluents, while weak acids are produced by dairies, fruit juice factories, breweries, and preservative factories, and they can also be found in bog waters or elsewhere.

A measure of the strength of an acid is its $p$H value. The lower the $p$H value (under $p$H 7), the more corrosive the acid.

Special mention should be made of carbonic acid, which readily dissolves limestone, as its ability to attack cannot be expressed by its $p$H value alone. It occurs partly as free carbonic acid, which is present in many waters, and partly from the maintenance of the limestone–carbon dioxide equilibrium. Even small quantities attack concrete. Carbonic acid acts like other weak acids, and is capable of dissolving lime from concrete;

$$CaCO_3 + H_2O + CO_2 \longrightarrow Ca(HCO_3)_2$$
calcium carbonate + carbon dioxide $\longrightarrow$ calcium bicarbonate
(limestone)

| | |
|---|---|
| sparingly soluble | very soluble |
| (solubility in water | (solubility in water |
| at 18°C, 13 mg/litre) | at 18°C, 1890 mg/litre) |

Carbonic acid is frequently found in soft waters, e.g., in areas where there are igneous rocks in the substrata. Particularly high concentrations are naturally to be expected in areas which contain carbonic acid springs (spas, etc.). Addition of limestone does not prevent this form of corrosion.

*Attack by salts with ion exchange properties*

Certain magnesium and ammonium salts (e.g., chlorides) react with the set cement (ammonium carbonate, oxalate, and fluoride do not react). They act as solvents because chloride, in particular, readily forms water soluble compounds with calcium hydroxide contained in the concrete. Magnesium compounds may separate as hydroxide (a soft, gel-like mass) either on the outside or inside, and can therefore cause swelling. Ammonia is released in the form of a gas.

*Attack by soft water*

The softer the water, the less calcium and magnesium salts it contains in solution. For this reason soft water can dissolve relatively large quantities of these salts from concrete. Very soft water (less than 1.1 milliequivalent total hardness) can attack the surface, but dense concrete which has been made correctly is resistant even to very soft water.

*Attack by fats and oils*

Normally only organic (plant and animal) fats and oils attack concrete. All contain smaller or larger quantities of free fatty acids, which, like other weak acids, attack concrete. In addition, the fatty acids can react with the calcium compounds contained in the set concrete with the formation of calcium salts (soaps) of the fatty acids and glycerol. This decomposition of the fat (saponification) causes a softening of the concrete. Mineral oils and fats, provided they contain no acids or resins, do not attack concrete. If concrete is completely impregnated with fats and oils its hardness and strength of adhesion to the steel reinforcement are impaired.

### 2.2.2 Attack by Swelling Action

If sulfate solutions penetrate into concrete, reactions may take place between parts of the set cement and the hydrates of calcium aluminate. These form voluminous new structures inside the concrete. The following equation gives an example of what happens:

$$3CaO \cdot Al_2O_3 + 3(CaSO_4 \cdot 2H_2O) + 26H_2O \longrightarrow$$
$$3CaO \cdot Al_2O_3 \cdot 3CaSO_4 \cdot 32H_2O$$

or

$$C_3A + 3(Cs \cdot 2H) + 26H \longrightarrow C_3A \cdot 3Cs \cdot 32H$$

tricalcium aluminate + gypsum + water $\longrightarrow$ trisulfate

Crystalline trisulfate, which is produced, has a very much larger volume than the solid starting materials because of the introduction of an appreciable quantity of water of crystallization. As the space it has to occupy is limited, it subjects its surroundings to pressure and therefore induces cracking.

This sulfate expansion can be avoided by using cements which contain little or no $C_3A$ (cf. section 2.2.4). With very high sulfate concentration (in excess of 1200 mg $SO_4^{2-}$/liter) it is possible for gypsum to separate from calcium hydroxide solution in the hardened concrete. This also causes swelling. Sulfate occurs in ground and effluent waters.

### 2.2.3   Other Types of Attack

Dissolving and swelling attacks are by far the most common. Other attacks are much rarer. For example, many organic materials (e.g., primary aliphatic esters such as methylacetate) are able to break up concrete. Only an expert can assess the likelihood of such reactions in specific cases.

### 2.2.4   Assessment of Chemical Attack

#### 2.2.4.1   Fundamentals

The degree of attack by waters and soils which have a harmful effect upon concrete depends on the type and concentration of the aggressive media concerned. Chemical reactions between the aggressive media and the set concrete occur at quite low concentrations. Experience shows, however, that it is only necessary to modify the building techniques if concentrations exceed certain limiting values. The observation of external phenomena such as odor and color does not suffice for a correct assessment. It is usually necessary to carry out a chemical analysis of a sample of water. Samples of river water, effluent water, groundwater, or seepage water from the subsoil are typical cases in point. The chemical analysis of a soil sample is only necessary if it is impossible to extract water samples, and then only when one suspects the presence in the ground of materials which attack concrete. Such suspicions arise, for example, with geological formations in which salts are present. (Zechstein, Triassic, Jurassic, Tertiary).

Moorlands, areas near garbage, slag heaps, and mine tails, as well as unusually colored soils, are also suspect (see table 2.1).

A chemical investigation to assess the chance of attack on concrete by waters and soils should determine the following:

*Analysis of waters*

1. $p$H
2. Odor
3. Potassium permanganate, mg $KMnO_4$/liter
4. Total hardness, milliequivalents/liter
5. Carbonate hardness, milliequivalents/liter
6. Noncarbonate hardness, milliequivalents/liter
7. Magnesium, mg $Mg^{2+}$/liter
8. Ammonium, mg $NH_4^+$/liter
9. Sulfate, mg $SO_4^{2-}$/liter
10. Chloride, mg $Cl^-$/liter
11. Carbonic acid, mg $CO_2$/liter (determined by means of the marble test, according to Heyer)

*Soil analysis*

1. Acidity according to Baumann-Gully
2. Sulfate, mg $SO_4^{2-}$/kg air dried soil
3. Sulfide in mg $S^{2-}$/kg air dried soil

DIN 4030 contains standard values of the concentrations for assessment of which aggressive media would be "normal." The aggressivity of a medium can, however, be increased under conditions of equal concentration by increasing the temperature, by alternate drying and wetting of the building component, and by rapid flow. It can also be reduced, e.g., if the aggressive media are brought into contact more slowly than is the case with soils which are more porous (penetration coefficient $< 10^{-5}$ meters/second).

### 2.2.4.2 The Nature of Attack by Water

The exact assessment depends on the results of a chemical analysis. Depending on the type and concentration of the aggressive medium, one can distinguish between three degrees of attack: weak, strong, and very strong. The following are considered to be of particular importance: $p$H, carbonic acid content ($H_2CO_3$), and the concentrations of

Table 2.3.   Harmful Components in Waters. *(Source: DIN 4030)*

| Harmful components | Concentration | | |
|---|---|---|---|
| | weak attack | strong attack | very strong attack |
| 1. Acids, $pH$ | 6.5–5.5 | 5.5–4.5 | < 4.5 |
| 2. $CO_2$ and $H_2CO_3$, mg/liter (Heyer marble test) | 15–30 | 30–60 | > 60 |
| 3. Ammonium ($NH_4^+$), mg/liter | 15–30 | 30–60 | > 60 |
| 4. Magnesium ($Mg^{2+}$), mg/liter | 200–300 | 300–1500 | > 1500 |
| 5. Sulfates ($SO_4^{2-}$), mg/liter | 200–600 | 600–3000 | > 3000 |

ammonium ($NH_4^+$), magnesium ($Mg^{2+}$), and sulfate ($SO_4^{2-}$) ions. The limiting values are given in Table 2.3, which is taken from DIN 4030. They apply for stagnant and slowly flowing natural waters, which are present in large quantities and are in direct contact with the concrete structure. The maximum rate of attack given in table 2.3 is always the one applicable. If two or more values lie in the upper quarter range— with $pH$ in the lower quarter—the attack is raised by one degree. With regard to $CO_2$ concentrations, new investigations by Sprung and Rechenberg have indicated that one can expect a strong attack only when the concentration is in excess of 100 mg $CO_2$/liter.

The smell which is observed (with alkaline waters only after addition of acid), and the $KMnO_4$ demand (degree of oxidation) show whether appreciable quantities of organic compounds, hydrogen sulfide or other sulfides are present. In doubtful cases, when for example there is a smell of hydrogen sulfide (rotten eggs) or when a filtered sample of water exhibits a $KMnO_4$ demand in excess of 50 mg/liter, the help of an expert is required. One would expect effluents to have high $KMnO_4$ demand values. In general, domestic effluents are not particularly corrosive to concrete, while industrial effluents are very corrosive. The degree of oxidation ($KMnO_4$ demand) is not a direct measure of aggressivity. The total hardness should show whether the surface of the concrete might be dissolved (as with very soft water). High chloride content can impair the corrosion protection of the reinforcement; under such circumstances it would be advisable to increase the thickness of concrete cover. Set concrete is not attacked by $Cl^-$.

*Seawater*

Seawater behaves exceptionally. The salt content of the oceans is about 36 g/liter. On the basis of a $Mg^{2+}$ content of 1330 mg/liter and

$SO_4^{2-}$ content of 2780 mg/liter, one might assume that seawater is very aggressive against concrete. Experience, however, shows that seawater has a low degree of attack in comparison with a pure magnesium sulfate solution of equal concentration. Building components made from dense concrete are stable in seawater, as shown by many decades of observation.

The reason for this is probably the formation of calcium carbonate on the surface of the concrete, which arises by the reaction of bicarbonate ions (145 mg $HCO_3^-$/liter) in seawater with calcium hydroxide in the set concrete. This calcium carbonate seals the concrete surface and thus prevents the penetration of aggressive substances.

Seawater can be classified as weakly aggressive, i.e., a dense concrete (maximum water penetration depth less than 30 mm) is stable against seawater independent of the type of cement used. Cements with high sulfate resistance should be used when the density of the concrete cannot be guaranteed.

### 2.2.4.3 The nature of attack by subsoils

Chemical analysis also serves to enable accurate evaluations of the degree of attack by soils to be made. Superficial examination such as color observation can only give a rough indication. The degree of attack of soils is only given as weak or strong. Table 2.4 gives limiting values for the assessment of soils which are frequently wetted.

Selection is governed by the highest degree of attack quoted. With decreasing porosity of the gound, the degree of aggressivity diminishes. In the case of soils where the sulfide content is more than 100 mg $S^{2-}$/kg of air dried soil, and in other special cases, such as buildings next to garbage dumps, it is necessary to obtain expert advice. The reason for this is that certain sulfides readily oxidize to sulfates.

Table 2.4. Harmful Components in Soils. (Source: DIN 4030)

| Harmful components | Concentration | |
|---|---|---|
| | Weak Attack | Strong Attack |
| 1. Acids, Baumann - Gully acidity | > 20 | — |
| 2. Sulfates, mg/kg of dry soil | 2000–5000 | > 5000 |

## 2.2.4.4   *The nature of attack by gases*

If aggressive components in concrete are enriched constantly, it is possible for damage to occur. Gas analysis and an assessment of the local conditions must be carried out by an expert.

### 2.2.5   Corrosion Protection of Set Cement in Concrete and Mortar

Aggressive waters and soils can be assessed and classified into different degrees of aggressivity. The resistance of concrete against chemical attack increases in general with increasing density, because this prevents the penetration of aggressive materials.

*Protection against weak and strong attacks*

All types of cement can be used, except where there is a likelihood of sulfate attack (see below). All usual cement ballasts can also be used, provided they withstand the aggressive medium (for exceptions, see section 2.3).

When there is weak and strong attack, it is sufficient to produce a concrete from the usual starting materials, but to increase its resistance by raising the density. The water penetration values permitted are given in Table 2.5. Concrete intended to resist weak or strong attacks should generally be grade B2. A dense concrete mix means a dense set cement, and for this reason maximum permissible water to cement ratios in relationship to the degree of attack, as shown in table 2.5, are obligatory. In building construction the water to cement ratios should,

**Table 2.5.   Formulation of Concrete to Counteract Chemical Attack.**
**(Source: DIN 4030)**

|  | Weak Attack | Strong Attack | Very Strong Attack |
|---|---|---|---|
| Minimum cement content, kg/m³ | 400 | | |
| Water to cement ratio | 0.6 | 0.5 | 0.5 |
| Water penetration depth, mm | 50 | 30 | 30 |
| Surface protection | — | — | necessary |
| Type of cement | When waters contain more than 400 mg $SO_4^{2-}$/liter, or when soils contain more than 3000 mg $SO_4^{2-}$/kg, the use of sulfate resistant cement is essential | | |
| Thickness of concrete cover over reinforcement | more than 30 mm | | |

if at all possible, be kept 0.05 lower than the recommended figure, so that no random single values stray over the permissible limiting ratio.

The fines content (cement and smallest particles $< 0.25$ mm) can affect the stability of the set concrete against chemical attacks. It should neither be too high nor too low. For this reason DIN 1045 specifies the following values for fines contents:

With   8 mm maximum ballast size, 525 kg/m$^3$ concrete
With 16 mm maximum ballast size, 450 kg/m$^3$ concrete
With 32 mm maximum ballast size, 400 kg/m$^3$ concrete
With 63 mm maximum ballast size, 325 kg/m$^3$ concrete

If the attack is only weak, one may produce the concrete for hardness classes up to and including Bn 250, according to conditions B1 even without previous suitability tests. It is, however, necessary that a minimum cement content be maintained, depending upon the maximum grain size, and that the size distribution range remains in the most suitable range between the standard sieve lines A and B.

It is necessary to be specially careful when laying, consolidating, and curing the concrete. The concrete must be uniform and completely consolidated. To avoid joints, which if present must be watertight, the building section should as far as possible be prepared in one single working operation. The concrete must be kept damp for at least 7 days.

*Protection against very strong attack*

With very strong attack, in addition to the measures which are needed for strong attack it is necessary to provide permanent protection of the concrete against direct exposure to aggressive media (DIN 4031, DIN 4117). The aggressive media must be kept away from the concrete completely.

Protective coatings made from bituminous materials and plastics, are attached by means of painting, rolling, spraying, or spatula application using either hot or cold techniques.

In the design and construction of the building one should take care that the areas which can be attacked should be as small as possible. Edges and corners should be rounded. Building areas should be enclosed, even, and inclined so as to facilitate the runoff of water. The concrete surfaces must be roughened prior to the application of the protective layers and cleaned. Unevennesses must be eliminated.

The protective coating must adhere well and be free from cracks,

## Table 2.6. Standard Values of the Resistance Characteristics of Fully Set Protective Coatings.[1]

Symbols: + resistant, (+) resistant under certain conditions, — nonresistant.

| a | b | c | d | e | f | g | h | i | k | l | m | n | o | p | q |
|---|---|---|---|---|---|---|---|---|---|---|---|---|---|---|---|
| | | Bituminous Materials[2] | | Polymer Varnishes | | | | Protective Coatings / Polymer Suspensions | | | Setting Plastics | | | Setting Plastics Blended With Pitch | |
| Group | Active Materials / Type | Bitumen | Pitch | Chlorinated Latex | PVC | Chlorosulfonic Polyethylene (CSP) | Polyvinylidine Chloride (PVDC) | PVC | Polystyrene | Acrylate and Methacrylate Co-polymers | Unsaturated Polyester Resin | Epoxy Resin | Polyurethane Resin | Epoxy Resin | Polyurethane Resin |
| 1 | Water up to 30°C, moor water, reactive $CO_2$, sulfate solutions, condensing salt solutions | + | + | + | + | + | + | + | + | + | + | + | + | + | + |
| 2 | Water between 30°C and 60°C | + | + | + | (+) | + | (+) | (+) | (+) | (+) | + | + | + | + | + |
| 3 | Solutions of ammonium salts | + | (+) | + | + | + | (+) | (+) | (+) | (+) | + | + | + | + | + |
| 4 | Dilute mineral acids (up to $pH$ 2) | + | + | (+) | (+) | + | + | (+) | (+) | (+) | + | (+) | (+) | + | + |
| 5 | Concentrated mineral acids | — | — | — | — | + | (+) | — | — | — | + | — | — | (+) | — |
| 6 | Low molecular weight organic acids | (+) | (+) | (+) | — | (+) | + | — | (+) | (+) | (+) | (+) | (+) | (+) | (+) |
| 7 | Fatty acids | — | (+) | (+) | (+) | (+) | (+) | + | + | + | + | (+) | (+) | (+) | (+) |

Water and materials which act as acids

20

| No. | Group | Material | 1 | 2 | 3 | 4 | 5 | 6 | 7 | 8 | 9 | 10 | 11 | 12 | 13 |
|---|---|---|---|---|---|---|---|---|---|---|---|---|---|---|---|
| 8 | Alkalis | Ammonia solutions | + | + | + | + | + | (+) | + | + | + | + | + | + | + |
| 9 | | Dilute alkalis (up to pH 13) | + | (+) | + | + | + | + | + | + | (+) | + | (+) | + | (+) |
| 10 | | Concentrated alkalis | − | − | (+) | (+) | + | (+) | (+) | + | (+) | + | + | + | − |
| 11 | Oils and fuels | Plant and animal fats and oils | − | − | − | + | + | + | + | + | + | + | + | + | + |
| 12 | | Lubricating oils | − | (+) | (+) | (+) | + | (+) | + | + | + | + | + | + | + |
| 13 | | Fuel oils³ | − | − | (+) | + | + | + | + | + | + | + | + | + | + |
| 14 | | Aliphatic hydrocarbons | − | − | (+) | + | − | + | + | + | (+) | + | + | + | + |
| 15 | | Aromatic hydrocarbons | − | − | − | − | − | − | (+) | + | − | − | + | + | + |
| 16 | | Heavy tar oils | − | − | − | − | (+) | − | − | − | − | − | − | − | − |
| 17 | | Mechanical wear | − | (+) | (+) | (+) | (+) | − | (+) | + | (+) | + | + | (+) | (+) |

¹If structure is exposed to ultraviolet radiation (sunlight) at the same time, "resistant under certain conditions" should be substituted for "resistant" in some cases.

²If structure is exposed to ultraviolet radiation (sunlight) at the same time, the minimum layer thickness should be 0.5 mm.

³Protective coatings intended for the internal protection of fuel tanks must comply with special specifications.

impermeable to the media which attack concrete, and sufficiently resistant against thermal, mechanical, biological and chemical actions. The coating must be capable of conforming to unavoidable deformations of the building components and able to bridge cracks up to about 0.2 mm in width. When protective coatings are applied care must be taken, that no less than the minimum thickness of the layer be reached anywhere (without mechanical stress, minimum = 0.2 mm; light to average mechanical stress, 1–3 mm; heavy mechanical stress, 3 mm). The protective coating should be dense and, as far as possible, its thickness should be constant. When coatings consist of several layers, each individual layer should have a different color. During application it is absolutely essential that the instructions of the manufacturers be followed regarding application time, ambient temperature, and relative humidity conditions.

Table 2.6 contains standard values of the properties of the most important protective coatings for concrete. Correct application and dense coats are assumed. The standard values are only a guide and do not apply in every single case. The compositions of the reacting resins may vary. The setting period and the setting temperature, as well as the concentration of the aggressive medium may also fluctuate. Active media also include those which can attack certain protective coatings but not concrete. To avoid trouble it is advisable to ask the manufacturer to confirm whether a given protective coating is resistant when used for a specific purpose.

*Sulfate attack*

To protect against attack by waters with more than 400 mg $SO_4^{2-}$/ liter and against soils with more than 3000 mg $SO_4^{2-}$/kg, cements with high sulfate resistance must be used. Such cements are Portland cements with less than 3% tricalcium aluminate ($C_3A$) by weight and less than 5% $Al_2O_3$ by weight, as well as blast furnace cements with more than 70% by weight of ground clinker.

## 2.3 DAMAGE DUE TO REACTIONS OF THE BALLAST

The ballast, which is usually silicate material, is generally more resistant to corrosion than the set cement. Exceptions have already been mentioned (limestone and dolomite can be attacked by acid waters; while certain types of mica can swell when sulfates are present). Harmful components are mud-forming substances, materials of organic origin, materials which interfere with the hardening process, sulfur compounds (sulfate swelling, see section 2.2.2), silicic acid, and materials which attack steel (see section 2.4.2).

*Alkali swelling*

If a concrete is made with ballast consisting of poorly crystallized or amorphous $SiO_2$ (silicon dioxide, which is also often called silicic acid), and cement rich in alkali, it is possible for alkali swelling to occur. This is caused by gel formation. Gels can swell because they absorb water. Alkali swelling causes a reduction in strength or complete destruction of the concrete. The following types of ballast are suspect: opal, flint, chalcedony, opal sandstone as well as silicic dolomite and limestone, silica and mica slate. If alkalis act on dolomite ballast which contains no free silicic acid, swelling phenomena can still occur.

**Table 2.7. Assessment of the Environmental Conditions Which Affect Alkaline Reactions.**

| Dry | Concrete building components which remain mainly dry in use, e.g., inside dwellings and, if there is proper protection against moisture, outside as well. |
|---|---|
| Moist | Concrete components which frequently remain damp for long periods of time, e.g., components used in bridge building, dam construction or foundations. |
| Moist, with external alkali exposure | Similar to "moist" but with external exposure to alkalis. Examples are long term exposure to seawater or basic salt solutions. |

**Table 2.8. Preventive Measures Against Destructive Alkali Reactions in Concrete.**

| | Preventive measures | | |
|---|---|---|---|
| Alkali sensitivity of ballast | dry conditions | moist conditions | moist conditions with external alkali exposure |
| completely inert | none | none | none |
| usable under certain conditions | none | low alkali cement[1] | low alkali cement |
| suspect | none | low alkali cement | change the ballast[2] |

[1]Only with concrete with a grading higher than Bn 350.
[2]Only with concrete with a grading higher than Bn 350. In other cases use low alkali cement.

**Table 2.9.   Assessment of Sensitivity of Ballast to Alkalis on the Basis of its Hydrated Amorphous Silica Sandstone Content, as Well as That of Other Stones Containing Hydrated Amorphous Silica and Reactive Flint.**

| Components | Limiting Values for Stages in Sensitivity, % by Weight | | |
|---|---|---|---|
| | Inert | Suitable Under Certain Conditions | Suspect |
| Sandstone and other rocks containing hydrated amorphous silica[1] (opal) | $< 0.5$ | 0.5–2.0 | $> 2.0$ |
| Reactive flint with diameter in excess of 4 mm | $< 3.0$ | 3.0–10.0 | $> 10.0$ |
| Mixture of 5 parts sandstone or other rocks containing hydrated amorphous silica to one part of reactive flint | $< 4.0$ | 4.0–15.0 | $> 15.0$ |

[1]Including reactive flint with diameters between 1 and 4 mm.

**Table 2.10.   Limiting Values for the Composition of Cements with Low Active Alkali Content.**

| | Total Alkali Content, % by Weight of $Na_2O$ Equivalent | Content of Ground Slag, % by Weight |
|---|---|---|
| Portland cement | $\leqslant 0.60$ | — |
| Blast furnace cement | $\leqslant 0.90$<br>2.00 | $\geqslant 50$<br>$\geqslant 65$ |

To avoid alkali swelling it is necessary to apply preventive treatment, which varies according to environmental conditions (Table 2.7 and Table 2.8). If the ballast is selected according to Table 2.9 and cement with low active alkali content is employed (Table 2.10), alkali swelling is most unlikely to take place.

## 2.4   CORROSION AND CORROSION PROTECTION OF REINFORCEMENT STEELS

### 2.4.1   Fundamentals

When cement is being hydrated, or to be more exact, when calcium silicate is being hydrated, calcium hydroxide [$Ca(OH)_2$] is formed.

This calcium hydroxide is partly dissolved in the water within the pores (supersaturated $Ca(OH)_2$ solution), and partly precipitated in the form of calcium hydroxide crystals, which are embedded within the set cement. This is the reason why most concretes have a $p$H value in excess of 12, i.e., they are strongly basic. In such a basic environment steel is made passive, i.e., it is protected from corrosion by means of an impervious protective layer of iron oxides.

If it can be ensured that this impervious, dense, protective layer is maintained on the entire surface of the reinforcement, there is no danger of corrosion taking place.

### 2.4.2  Corrosion of Reinforcement Steels

There are, however, situations when this corrosion protection is lost. If, in addition, moisture and oxygen come into contact with the steel, rust formation will occur. The following are the conditions under which corrosion of steel in concrete can take place.

1. Faults in the concrete (tears, cracks, agglomerations of sand, etc.) can prevent the steel from being made passive in certain positions.
2. The protective calcium hydroxide $Ca(OH)_2$ can take up $CO_2$ from the air with time and form calcium carbonate (carbonation). This reaction corresponds to the hardening of slaked lime:

$$Ca(OH)_2 + CO_2 + H_2O \longrightarrow CaCO_3 + 2H_2O$$

It proceeds from the outside to the inside. Inside the carbonated concrete the $p$H-value falls to somewhat below 9.* This takes place when the $CO_2$ concentration of air amounts to 0.03% by volume. When the $p$H value is below 10, the corrosion protection of the steel is no longer assured. The steel can rust and in consequence loses its strength. Because rusted steel increases in volume it may cause the concrete cover to crack. Corrosion of nontensioned reinforcement steel does not, however, occur in every case, but depends upon environmental conditions. High

---

*This condition can be determined easily by applying phenolphthalein indicator to a freshly broken surface of the concrete. When the $p$H is greater than 9, the color is red; when it is less than 9, the indicator is colorless. Carbonated sections therefore appear colorless, while noncarbonated ones are red.

tensile strength steels, however, are very sensitive and must never be positioned in the carbonated layer.

The rate of carbonation is mainly influened by the following:

a. *Humidity.* The rate of carbonation is a maximum at 50–70% relative humidity, while under water it equals zero.

b. *The composition of the concrete,* particularly the water to cement ratio. As the water to cement ratio rises a more porous structure develops. Carbonation rates increase as follows with increasing water to cement ratios:

  If the rate of carbonation is 1 when the water to cement ratio is 0.6, the rate is 2 with a water to cement ratio of 0.8 but only 0.4 when the water to cement ratio is 0.45. Portland cement concrete carbonates more slowly than blast furnace cement concrete.

c. *Curing:* If concrete is kept moist for a longer period of time, its resistance against carbonation increases.

d. *Time:* At constant temperature and average humidity the progress of carbonation is roughly proportional to the square root of time, i.e., with increasing time the rate of carbonation falls. When concrete is completely wetted through, carbonation stops altogether. Depths of carbonation of roughly 40 mm have been observed with concrete about 50 years old.

3. Under the action of halides, particularly chlorides, it is possible for reinforcement steel to corrode at certain positions even if it has been positioned correctly within a basic environment. Encrustations and holes may appear in the steel (pitting corrosion). Corrosion is only induced by *free* chloride ions. Chlorides which are part of hydrated ions, as for example, the hydrate of calcium aluminate chloride, are harmless. Destructive effects have been noted, for example, after the burning of PVC (polyvinylchloride) stores, because gaseous hydrochloric acid was liberated.

4. The following types of corrosion occur only with high tensile steels.

a. *Stress corrosion.* This is a tearing effect, which may be inter- or intracrystalline, of a metallic material due to the simultaneous action of tensile stresses and a corrosive agent (e.g., chlorides or nitrates). High tensile stresses occur at corrosion scars to cause fractures, without anything being visible from the outside.

b. *Hydrogen embrittlement.* Sulfides, which are present in clay and blast furnace cement, can lead to the formation of hydrogen sulfide ($H_2S$), which forms hydrogen in the presence of steel. As this is only possible when the $p$H is below 9, hydrogen embrittlement should not occur with any properly prepared cement or with blast furnace cement. Clay cement is, however, vulnerable.

Atomic hydrogen, which is liberated in the decomposition of $H_2S$, can penetrate into the crystal lattice of steel because of its small atomic radius. If it reaches grain interfaces or faults, it causes a change in properties. Plastic properties, in particular, are affected extremely unfavorably, and cracking can take place. The energy required is provided by the hydrogen, as it changes from the atomic state to the molecular state.

### 2.4.3 Corrosion Protection of Reinforcement Steels

The concrete cover of reinforcement steels and stirrups must at no point be less than the values given in Tables 2.11 and 2.12. In special cases the concrete cover must be increased, e.g., when the maximum size of the ballast is in excess of 32 mm, when concrete is in constant

Table 2.11. Minimum Concrete Cover as a Function of the Diameter of the Reinforcement Steel. *(Source: DIN 1045)*

| Diameter of Rods, mm | Concrete Cover, mm |
|:---:|:---:|
| $\leqslant 12$ | 10 |
| 14 16 18 | 15 |
| 20 22 | 20 |
| 25 28 | 25 |
| $> 28$ | 30 |

**Table 2.12. Minimum Thickness of Concrete Cover, Depending on Environmental Conditions, mm. (Source DIN 1045)**

| 1 | 2 | 3 | 4 | 5 | 6 |
|---|---|---|---|---|---|
| | Concrete Grade | | | | |
| | Bn 150 | | ≥ Bn 250 | | |
| Environmental Conditions | General | Loadbearing Sections[1] | General | Loadbearing Sections[1] | Factory Produced Precast Sections |
| 1. Building components in enclosed areas, e.g., in dwellings (including kitchen, bathroom, and laundry room), offices, schools, hospitals, shops, etc., unless other factors, mentioned below, come into play.<br><br>Building components which remain constantly under water, or are kept permanently dry.<br><br>Roofs which are covered by a waterproof skin, for the side on which the skin is positioned. | 20 | 15 | 15 | 10 | 10 |
| 2. Building components in the open air and building components which are permanently exposed to outside air, e.g., open sheds or even lock-up garages. | 25 | 20 | 20 | 15 | 15 |

| No. | Description | | | | | |
|---|---|---|---|---|---|---|
| 3. | Building sections in enclosed areas with frequent very high relative humidity at ordinary room temperature, e.g., in public kitchens, public baths, laundries, damp areas of indoor swimming pools, and in stables. | 30 | 25 | 25 | 20 | 20 |
| | Building sections subjected to differing degrees of damp, e.g., in areas with strong condensation or changes of damp exposure. | | | | | |
| | Building components which are subjected to weak chemical attack. | | | | | |
| 4. | Building components which are exposed to particularly severe corrosive action (e.g., permanent exposure to aggressive gases or salts) as well as strong chemical attack. | 40 | 35 | 35 | 30 | 30 |

[1]Loadbearing sections referred to in this table are slabs, corrugated roofing sections, floor and roof slabs, shells, folded sections and walls.

contact with water, and for washed and sandblasted areas. Under particularly corrosive environmental conditions (Table 2.12, line 4) other protective measures such as external protecting layers should also be considered.

Because of the danger of chloride attack, the $Cl^-$ content must not exceed 0.1% by weight in the cement and 0.1% by weight in the ballast in the case of prestressed concrete. For normal reinforced concrete the figure is 0.2% by weight. Blast furnace cement must contain less than 50% by weight of ground slag. Corrosive attack can also be prevented by the use of protective paint coatings on the concrete; for example, epoxy resin has proven effective against chloride attack.

No additional protection of the reinforcement is normally necessary. Three types of protective measures are being used for special circumstances although opinions regarding their utility are by no means unanimous:

1. Zinc coatings on reinforcement steels have been used successfully in many countries.
2. Layers of synthetic resins on the reinforcement steels are employed.
3. Inhibitors are added to concrete.

Special measures are used when dealing with the reinforcement irons for light-weight concretes which have closed pores. In the case of expanded polystyrene concrete with closed pores, corrosion protection is improved nowadays by dipping the steel into hydraulic cement. There is a greater danger of corrosion when aerated or foamed concrete is used than when concrete with closed pores is used, because in the former cases the $p$H is appreciably lower and the pores are mostly not completely filled with water, so that oxygen is able to penetrate easily. Hence the reinforcement in aerated or foamed concretes must have special additional corrosion protection, such as hydraulic cement mixed with latex or bituminous materials.

# 3
# CORROSION AND CORROSION PROTECTION OF CERAMIC BUILDING MATERIALS

The building industry uses almost exclusively silicate ceramic materials. These offer good resistance against aggressive media. They are also absolutely resistant to chemical action from the atmosphere. With reduced porosity, which is usually achieved by employing higher burning temperatures, which can go up to sintering levels during production, the stability increases. Building bricks are usually heated, today, to about 950–1150°C, while engineering bricks are burned at about 1050–1250°C. The porosity of building bricks is about 20–40%, while that of engineering bricks is 5–10%. In consequence, the resistance of engineering bricks against acids and alkalis is appreciably higher. Glazing further increases corrosion resistance. Because of their good resistance to many chemicals, ceramics are also widely used in the building of laboratories and in the chemical industry.

Normal bricks, engineering bricks, and other ceramic products must be free of swelling components, such as lumps of unreacted lime and other materials (especially magnesium sulfate) which may cause flaking off or destructive leaching phenomena. Facing bricks and engineering bricks must not contain any salts which may permanently mar the appearance of unplastered wall surfaces. High grade masonary bricks with a maximum of 0.06% by weight of magnesium sulfate, as tested on a fresh sample, should prove troublefree. If the total sodium sulfate and potassium sulfate content is less than 0.04% by weight, no permanent deterioration of the appearance of the visible surfaces would be expected.

Ceramic clinker should also possess good resistance against all acids except hydrofluoric acid, and good resistance against alkalis. The same is true for various clinker tiles and ceramic tiles. Good acid resistance is offered by materials which contain a high percentage of crystalline $SiO_2$, a low percentage of $Al_2O_3$ (about 20−30%), a densely sintered structure and, in consequence, a low capacity to absorb water. Test samples are dipped at room temperature into 70% sulfuric acid and into 20% potassium hydroxide. Any microscopic changes on the surface are then determined. The test is positive if observation of the surface through a microscope shows no visible change. Acid and alkali resistances can also be obtained on pulverized samples by evaluating weight losses. In the case of clinker bricks for the construction of acid resistant structures, the relative weight loss must not exceed 3%. Floor tiles must withstand domestic chemicals, acid and alkaline cleaning materials, bathwater, and acids and alkalis of concentrations below 20% by weight. Some chemical stoneware tiles comply with special specifications. Glazes should be immune to patch formation and resistant to organic solvents.

Pipelines and other shaped sections made from stoneware and their glazes are not attacked by effluents, groundwater, or any other substances likely to be present in soils, with the exception of hydrofluoric acid. If required, their corrosion resistances can be confirmed by tests similar to those used with clinker tiles. The loss in weight must not exceed 0.5% by mass.

Ceramic building materials usually do not induce corrosion in other building materials, as they are extremely inert.

# 4
# CORROSION AND
# CORROSION PROTECTION
# OF GLASS

Although glass is exceedingly inert to most media, it is not completely unaffected by moisture and chemicals. Its resistance to atmospheric action is governed mainly by its chemical composition. A high alkali content lowers the resistance, while high silicic acid and clay contents improve it. Water induces swelling, which is not visible to the naked eye. It causes a separation of the alkali lime silicate phase into alkali and alkaline earth hydroxides and silica gel. Hot water has a more drastic affect than cold water. This is hardly noticeable when it takes place at low temperatures and for brief periods of time, as is the normal circumstance. If, however, this reaction occurs in areas where there is constant contact with hot saturated air (swimming pools, greenhouses, factories), it may cause the glass surface to cloud. This is due to the formation of a surface layer of insoluble hydrated alkali lime silicate and silica gel. These phenomena can be seen particularly well when the alkalis which are produced (in this case alkali and alkaline earth hydroxide solutions) cannot be washed away. Instead their concentration increases with longer periods of exposure, as when sheet glass is packed damp without separating paper layers. If the hydroxides are washed away, e.g., by rainwater, the silica gel which remains forms a protective layer against further reaction processes.

Glass is resistant to acids (except hydrofluoric acid) and acid and neutral salt solutions. It is not, however, resistant to alkalis. The aggressivity of alkalis increases with concentration and temperature. Building glass is virtually never damaged by biological action. It is not common in the building industry to protect glass against corrosion.

# 5
# CORROSION AND CORROSION PROTECTION OF OTHER NONMETALLIC INORGANIC BUILDING MATERIALS

## 5.1 NATURAL STONES

Natural stones are used nowadays mainly for facing. For this reason their behavior in the atmosphere is of particular interest. Table 5.1 gives the weather resistance of important natural stones. The values for water absorption are also included, because they govern the penetration of aggressive solutions, and resistance to frost.

The suitability of natural stones for use in the building industry is mainly governed by their structure. Density, the adhesion of the mineral components to each other, and composition are of predominant importance. High porosity and cracks lower the quality of the stones. Igneous materials possess the best stability, and they exhibit almost indefinite durability in the atmosphere. These silicate stones are also very resistant to acids. An exception are certain basalts, called sunstones, which exhibit light gray spots after long exposure to air and gradually disintegrate.

Sedimentary materials show partly very good weather resistance, e.g., sandstone with silicate binder, dense graywackes, and dense limestone. Sandstones with clay content have a loose structure (montmorrillonite clay can swell by water absorption) and are therefore unsuitable; sandstones which contain lime as a binder are

## Table 5.1. Weather Resistance of Important Natural Rocks.

| Type of Rock | Density, $kg/m^3$ | Water Absorption, % by Weight | Stability |
|---|---|---|---|
| Igneous rocks | | | |
| Basalt | 2800–3100 | 0.1–0.3 | good, except nephelite |
| Diabase | 2800–2900 | 0.1–0.4 | good |
| Quartz porphyrite, rhyolite, porphyrite, andesite, keratophyrite, trachyte | 2500–2800 | 0.2–0.7 | good |
| Granite, syenite | 2600–2800 | 0.2–0.5 | very good; harmed when pyrites are present |
| Gabbro | 2800–3100 | 0.2–0.4 | very good, but made worse with increasing content of olivine and plagioclase |
| Diorite | 2700–3000 | 0.2–0.4 | good, but pyrites content is unfavorable |
| Limestone (dense) | 2650–2850 | 0.2–0.6 | good, but not acid resistant |
| Limestone (other types) | 1700–2600 | 0.2–10 | less good, not acid resistant |
| Sandstone (quartz bonding) | 2600–2650 | 0.2–0.5 | good |
| Sandstone (no quartz bonding) | 2000–2650 | 0.2–10 | mostly not stable |
| Metamorphic rocks | | | |
| Gneiss | 2650–3000 | 0.1–0.6 | mostly not stable |
| Mica slate | 2600–2800 | 0.1–0.8 | mostly not stable |
| Roof slate | 2700–2800 | 0.5–0.6 | good |

also far less durable. Pure silicate sedimentary rocks, particularly quartzite (dense sandstone with silica binder) are very resistant to acids, while limestone rocks, naturally, are not. Metamorphic rocks, like gneiss and mica slate, easily weather in the atmosphere. Other representatives of this group such as marble and metamorphic quartzite are weather resistant.

Some common reasons for the destruction of natural stone are temperature change (varying coefficients of thermal expansion of different mineral fractions cause internal stresses), frost damage (when water changes to ice, it increases in volume by about 10%), and erosion by wind loaded with solid particles. Water in particular, with its varying content of dissolved aggressive constituents, is an important destructive influence; for this reason, stability against chemical action is determined largely by water absorptivity. Dense stones have greater stability. Natural stones containing limestone are influenced by chemical action in the same way as artificial stones. Water containing dissolved carbon dioxide leaches out limestone (as well as dolomite), while water containing sulfuric acid changes the calcium carbonate to gypsum, thus causing the stone to pulverize and loosen, as well as to swell. This second reaction is becoming of particular importance nowadays, because of the appreciable loading of our atmosphere with $SO_2$. It is an important reason for the fact that buildings which are many hundreds of years old have weathered considerably in the last few decades.

When natural stone weathers, biological influences are also of importance. Algae and lichens can spread over the surfaces and exude acids. These are able to dissolve or roughen the surface of the stone. Because they are able to store water, lichens also further frost damage. If algae and lichen deposition takes place for longer periods of time, it becomes possible for higher plants, mostly mosses, to take root on the surface of the stone and to continue destruction. In addition, deposits of bird excrement are also chemically aggressive.

To avoid damage it is necessary to choose the right stone and to build correctly. Layered stones are laid in such a way that the natural grain lies horizontally, as this reduces rain penetration. Alternate soaking and drying, as well as frost, must be avoided with porous stones. It is necessary to provide good drainage.

The major attack usually occurs on the weather side. Polished stones resist weather better, as their surface offers fewer points of attack than a rough surface.

Capillary rise of groundwater in stone and subsequent evaporation above ground, which may happen with, for example, badly insulated sandstone walls, must be avoided. Otherwise there is a chance of dissolution, encrustation, and loosening inside the stonework, as well as the formation of encrustations, leaching out, and abrasion of the surface. The extent to which this takes place depends on the type of stone and the composition of the groundwater.

Natural stones can be protected against the influence of the weather by chemical treatment. It is, however, not possible to make an already weathered and embrittled stone completely resistant to atmospheric action by the use of protection media. It is difficult to assess protection media, because several decades of use are needed for valid results. Protection media for stone which seal the surface and thereby stop humidity exchange (e.g., oil paints) are unsuitable. Media which consolidate the grains of the entire rock structure, inside as well as out, have the best chance of success. Two methods of protection are given here. Both are used with concrete.

Fluoridation is carried out with 20–25% solutions of salts of fluorosilicic acid, $H_2SiF_6$ (mostly also containing $MgSiF_6$). The stones are impregnated or painted with these solutions. The salt solutions react with lime to form practically insoluble and chemically resistant compounds, according to the following equation:

$$MgSiF_6 + 2CaCO_3 \longrightarrow 2CaF_2 + MgF_2 + SiO_2 + 2CO_2$$

The new formations reduce porosity at the same time. If rocks which are free of lime or have a very low lime content are to be protected, it is necessary to pretreat with a dilute waterglass solution; this solution reacts inside the rocks with the fluorosilicate to form virtually completely insoluble and corrosion resistant compounds.

Silicone impregnation prevents the penetration of moisture (e.g., rainwater) into the building material, yet permits water vapor to pass. Silicone impregnation, when correctly formulated and applied, can offer the advantages of nonadhesive drying (so that no dust can collect), considerable depth of penetration, long durability (usually in excess of 10 years), and good resistance to ultraviolet rays. Solar radiation only acts very slowly. A further advantage is considerable alkali resistance, which is necessary in protection of stonework against mortar and concrete. Silicones are usually sprayed on under low pressure and are able to bridge hairline cracks of up to 0.3 mm.

## 5.2 ASBESTOS CEMENT AND AERATED CONCRETE

Asbestos cement (or, better, asbestos concrete) and aerated concrete contain cements as binders. Aerated concrete also usually contains lime. Their resistance to aggressive materials is, on the whole, similar to that of normal concrete. Asbestos cement, however, is denser than normal concrete, while aerated concrete is less dense, or more porous. For this reason aggressive media are less effective against asbestos cement, and more effective against aerated concrete. These building materials are also attacked by organic and inorganic acids in solutions with a $pH$ less than 6.5. Animal and plant oils and fats, carbonic acid, solutions of ammonium and magnesium salts, and sulfates of more than a minimum concentration, all attack these materials. Warm distilled water and hot condensation water also act as solvents when these materials are exposed to them for long periods of time.

Protective means similar to those used with normal concrete can be employed, e.g., application of paints with bitumen pitch or synthetic resin vehicle. It is also possible to add inhibitors. Asbestos cement water pipes are protected by means of disodium hydrogen phosphate, which forms an insoluble calcium phosphate protective layer. This provides resistance against carbonic acid. Steel reinforcement inside aerated concrete must receive special protection. Both asbestos cement and aerated concrete are practically immune to biological actions.

## 5.3 SILICATE CONCRETE AND CALCIUM SILICATE STONE

The resistance of silicate concrete and calcium silicate stonework against aggressive solutions is usually high. Porous and more permeable varieties are corroded more strongly than denser types.

Simple chemical attack by natural waters, e.g., groundwater and bog water, is mostly only slight. Many salt solutions (e.g., $MgCl_2$, $NaNO_3$, $Na_2SO_4$, $CaCl_2$) also have no effect. On the other hand, seawater, mineral oil, heavy fuel oil, and solutions of NaCl and $NH_4Cl$, etc. reduce the strength of these materials. Acids and alkalis such as hydrochloric acid and sodium hydroxide cause heavy corrosion even at low concentrations (around 1%). They induce erosion, and, when they are more concentrated, produce deep pitting, or spalling of external surfaces.

Special mention should be made of strong corrosion by acetic acid, which is very noticeable at concentrations below 1%. The binder is dissolved, so that only the sand remains. As acetic acid is produced by many organic oxidation, fermentation and rotting processes (in milk, beer, sewage, silage, etc.), particular attention must be paid to this agent in agricultural and industrial applications.

All this applies when the material is in permanent contact with the aggressive medium. Sometimes the materials are subjected to a low concentration salt solution, such as seawater, and are then dried out, the process being repeated over and over again. Even salts which are normally nonaggressive can then cause serious corrosion and appreciably reduce the strength of the material. The surfaces are leached out and abraded, while edges and corners corrode away. Apart from chemical attack, salt spalling destruction is, in such cases, particularly harmful. The crystallization of salt inside the structure produces high pressures. This can be seen, for example, in walls with rising damp.

In order to protect against corrosion, the penetration and subsequent evaporation of solutions must be avoided as much as possible. Painting and coating can be used in the same way as with concrete. Corrosion of unprotected steel reinforcement in silicate concrete can occur as calcium hydroxide reacts to form hydrated calcium silicate, and as carbonation proceeds. See section 2.4.2. regarding the rate of carbonation with respect to time, porosity etc.

## 5.4 GYPSUM, ANHYDRITE CEMENT, SLAKED LIME MORTAR, AND MAGNESIA MORTAR

Gypsum is used as plaster and cement in the inside of dwellings because of its sensitivity to water. Where long term dampness or permanently moisture saturated air are expected, neither gypsum nor anhydrite mortars should be used. However, it is possible to use these materials in places where there is only a *periodic* high relative humidity, e.g., in domestic bathrooms and kitchens. Gypsum should only be used as an external wall material if all dampness can be permanently excluded. Special construction techniques, e.g., well ventilated cladding panels made from weather resistant building materials (plastics, asbestos cement, aluminium and other sheets), as well as such building protection media as silicone emulsions, are employed for this purpose. Under the action of moisture gypsum gradually dissolves and the gypsum solution is sucked up by the building component; the water then evaporates. Crystallization of gypsum in the pores of the plaster, the strength of which has already been lowered by being wetted, now causes the structure to be loosened, and eventually to break up.

In contrast to lime and cement, gypsum does not prevent rusting, and for this reason metal lath and other metal components must be protected against corrosion. Gypsum must not be mixed with cement, as sulfate swelling can occur when the set concrete gets wet later on (see section 2.2.2).

Hydraulic mortars are practically completely water resistant after setting, but are soluble in acid. Their volume must remain constant, which means that after setting they should not contain any unbound CaO.

Magnesia cements, which are mostly used for flooring finishes, should never be exposed to either steady draughts or large temperature changes. It is most important to avoid relative air humidities higher than 75% or lower than 55%. They possess only a limited water resistance and for this reason it is recommended that hydrophobic floor cleaners be used. As magnesium salts attack concrete (see section 2.2.1) it is necessary to protect the concrete underneath the flooring finish with a coating of bituminous paint or similar material. It is also necessary to protect steel parts (e.g., reinforcements in reinforced concrete underneath the magnesia floor, water lines, etc.) against attack by magnesia binders (sulfates and chlorides; see section 6.1.5.) by means of paint finishes and similar materials.

# 6
# CORROSION AND
# CORROSION PROTECTION
# OF BUILDING METALS

## 6.1. CORROSION OF METALS USED IN BUILDING

### 6.1.1 General Observations

The term *corrosion* has already been explained in the introduction. The basic process of metal corrosion is quite simple: metallic atoms go into solution or form compounds as positively charged ions; the corroded metal is oxidized.

All building metals are made from ores, i.e. from stable, energy deficient, natural metal compounds, by the addition of energy (metallurgy). The pure metals which have been produced in this way are in an unstable, energy rich state which, according to the laws of thermodynamics, tends to revert to the energy deficient, stable, original state. This state is reached by means of corrosion processes, in which energy is liberated. Thus, rust corresponds in its chemical state to iron ore (limonite). To prevent such natural, spontaneous processes constant maintenance work is necessary; only in this way can a steel structure be adequately protected against corrosion and its value maintained.

Corrosion is caused by contact with aqueous solutions, air and its impurities, gases, various types of soils, other building materials, and many other chemical compounds. Metallic corrosion can be classified according to the following sets of criteria:

1. *Environmental conditions.* Environmental actions serve to produce or further corrosion in the atmosphere, in the ground, and in waters.
2. *External appearance.* As the external appearance often indicates the origins and types of corrosion, it makes good sense to subdivide accordingly, e.g., surface corrosion, pitting corrosion, intercrystalline corrosion.
3. *Combinations of chemical and mechanical action.* It is significant that chemical and mechanical actions which separately produce at worst moderate damage can cause extremely strong corrosion when acting together. Such changes in the properties of materials produced by a combination of mechanical and chemical actions are stress corrosion and fretting corrosion.
4. *The mechanism of corrosion.* It is necessary to distinguish between purely *chemical corrosion* processes, as for example, the oxidation or the dissolution of metals, and *electrochemical* corrosion processes. In the case of electrochemical corrosion processes, two metallic phases are connected by an electric conductor, while an electrolyte (a liquid which conducts electricity because of the presence of ions) is also present. Corrosion by stray currents in the ground also belongs in this group.

The most important mechanisms of corrosion are explained below. Subsequent sections are arranged according to the type of corrosion inducing environment.

### 6.1.1.1 Chemical corrosion reactions

Metals have a tendency to combine with oxygen to form oxides. This tendency is the stronger the less noble the metal (see section 6.1.1.2, below). The layers of oxide on the metal surface which are formed even in dry air may be insoluble and stable against an aqueous medium in contact with them. If this should be the case, and if at the same time the oxide layers are dense and adhere well to the metal, they prevent further attack and act as a corrosion prevention layer. An example of this is aluminum oxide. Iron differs in that, although it does form a surface oxide layer, this layer is loose and enables oxidation to proceed into the depth of the metal.

Chemical corrosion also takes place by the action of acids and alkalis on metals. Hydrochloric acid, for example, reacts with iron,

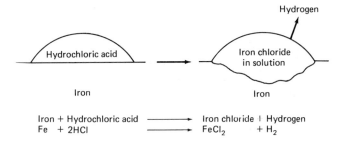

Iron + Hydrochloric acid         Iron chloride ⏐ Hydrogen
Fe  + 2HCl                  $FeCl_2$       $+ H_2$

**Figure 6.1.** Chemical corrosion as shown by acid attack.

and sodium hydroxide with aluminum (Figure 6.1.). If soluble reaction products are formed, the reaction only ends when either the aggressive medium, or the building metal are used up; if salts are formed which are sparingly soluble, they can form protective layers (sulfuric acid/lead).

### 6.1.1.2 Electrochemical corrosion reactions

Electrochemical corrosion is far more important than chemical corrosion. This type of corrosion takes place when two metallic phases with different electrochemical potentials are connected to each other by means of an electric conductor. Electrolytes such as acids, alkalis, salt solutions, or even milder media (e.g., rainwater, river water, groundwater, or tap water) also need to be present. Metallic phases with different electrochemical potentials exhibit electric potential differences. Potential differences may also arise because of impurities, agglomeration, internal stresses, corrosion products, damaged protective coatings, etc. They also occur when different metals are used in a building component (differential metals section 6.1.1.2.1, below). The larger the potential difference, the faster the rate of corrosion. The electrochemical EMF series (Table 6.1) gives the electrochemical potential of metals under normal conditions with respect to hydrogen (hydrogen is 0). The farther two metals in the electrochemical series are apart, the larger the potential difference

**Table 6.1. Electrochemical Potential Series, Volts.**

| K | Ca | Mg | Al | Zn | Cr | Fe | Ni | Sn | Pb | H | Cu | Ag | Au |
|---|----|----|----|----|----|----|----|----|----|---|----|----|----|
| −2.92 | −2.84 | −2.38 | −1.66 | −0.76 | −0.71 | −0.44 | −0.24 | −0.14 | −0.13 | 0.00 | +0.34 | +0.80 | +1.42 |

not noble   ——————————→ noble

Likelihood of passing into solution decreases from left to right.

between them. A metal is said to be less noble than those which stand to its right in the electrochemical series. In the case of electrochemical corrosion it is always the less noble metal which is removed. The potential difference does not, however, always fully correspond with the corrosion phenomena experienced in practice. The reason is that oxides and other metal compounds have differing electrochemical potentials.

*6.1.1.2.1 Differential metal corrosion*

Wherever two different metals or even two different types of the same metal (e.g., cast iron and wrought iron) are in contact, differential metal corrosion can take place. Such corrosion, however, only occurs in the presence of both oxygen and water.

In all cases of corrosion of this type the less noble metal becomes the anode of the electrolytic cell which is produced, while the nobler metal or alloy eliminates the electrons and hydrogen ions produced. The hydrogen ions are oxidized to water by means of the atmospheric oxygen present; in fact, the cathodic reaction is the rate determining step of the corrosion process. This is why a system with a large cathode and a small anode (e.g., a sheet of brass with steel bolts) induces extremely rapid corrosion of the steel. *One must never use a system of a small surface area of steel in conjunction with large areas of a more noble metal in corrosive circumstances* (Figure 6.2).

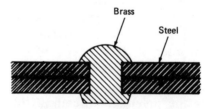

Satisfactory Design: Small cathode and large anode.

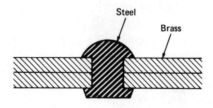

Unsatisfactory Design: Small anode and large cathode.

**Figure 6.2.** Differential metal corrosion.

If the cathode area is small, e.g., if one uses brass rivets to hold steel sheets together, the rate of corrosion is low because the rate determining step of the corrosion reaction is the speed at which the hydrogen ions of the corrosion reaction are oxidized. In this case only the minute surface area of the rivets is available, and this means that the rate of corrosion is very slow. The reactions which take place are as follows:

*On the anode:*

$$Fe \longrightarrow Fe^{2+} + 2 \text{ electrons}$$
$$2H_2O \longrightarrow 2OH^- + 2H^+$$
$$Fe^{2+} + 2OH^- \longrightarrow Fe(OH)_2 \text{ (rust)}$$

*On the cathode:*

$$2H^+ + \tfrac{1}{2}O_2 + 2 \text{ electrons} \longrightarrow H_2O$$

*6.1.1.2.2 Differential oxygenation corrosion*

Even if the base metal is uniform, different electrical potentials can be induced at different sections of the metal, if there are different concentrations of oxygen in contact with these sections. This is why a piece of steel covered by a defective paint film has a tendency to corrode. What happens is that the area in ready contact with air becomes the cathode, while the part covered by the paint becomes the anode. This is the reason for so called creeping corrosion, where rust formation creeps underneath paint films, cracked vitreous enamel, etc. (See Figure 6.3.)

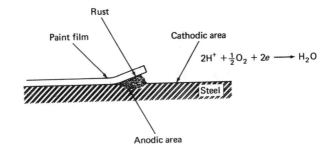

**Figure 6.3.** Creeping corrosion at the edges of paint films.

## 6.1.2   Atmospheric Corrosion

### *6.1.2.1   General observations*

Atmospheric corrosion can take place in the open air or in enclosed spaces. Atmospheric corrosion rates in the open air are increased by rain, high relative air humidity, and impurities. All these factors can fluctuate considerably from place to place and time to time, which is why corrosion rates vary so much. The average relative air humidity in many areas is higher in winter (80−95%) than in summer (60−80%). In consequence there is more corrosion in winter. Iron, for example, rusts five times as fast in winter as it does in summer.

Impurities in air influence the rate of corrosion more strongly than humidity. Such impurities are, in particular, dust, sulfur dioxide ($SO_2$), chlorine ($Cl_2$), ammonia ($NH_3$), nitrogen dioxide ($NO_2$), and hydrogen sulfide ($H_2S$).

Table 6.2 gives the impurities in city air. Although dust is, in terms of quantity, in first position, it has little effect on external corrosion. Building limestone dust and cement can attack aluminum in the presence of moisture, but most dusts do little harm, as they are chemically inert. The most important component of atmospheric pollution is $SO_2$, which is produced when fossil fuels burn, and which, particularly in winter, can achieve a very high concentration. With many metals the $SO_2$ content of air is directly related to the rate of corrosion. In coastal areas the salt concentrations, particularly the chloride content, plays an important part. Corrosion is particularly bad within the spray range at the seashore. With increasing distance from the source of pollution the impurities contained in air diminish and in consequence corrosion is reduced. According to Meller and co-

**Table 6.2.   Impurities in City Air. *(Source: Kutzelnigg)***

| Material | Average value, mg/m$^3$ | High value, mg/m$^3$ |
|---|---|---|
| Dust | 2.3 | 1000 |
| $SO_2$ | 0.8 | 50 |
| $Cl_2$ | 0.032 | |
| $NH_3$ | 0.045 | 0.68 |
| $NO_2$ | 0.001 | 0.025 |
| $H_2S$ | 0.001 | 10 |

**Table 6.3. Corrosion Losses of Building Metals in the Open Air, microns/year (approximate standard values)**

| Atmosphere | Aluminum | Lead | Iron, steel | Copper | Zinc |
|---|---|---|---|---|---|
| Industrial air | 0.7 | 0.7 | 40–170 | 1.3 | 3–22 |
| City air | 0.8 | 0.4 | 30–70 | 1.3 | 2–7 |
| Sea air | 0.7 | 0.5 | 60–200 | 1.4 | 1–7 |
| Country air | 0.05 | 0.4 | 10–65 | 0.5 | 1–2 |

workers, the sulfur dioxide content of air amounted to the following values, with increasing distances from the city center of St. Louis, Missouri: 0.8 km—0.32 g/m$^3$; 12 km—0.14 g/m$^3$; 28 km—0.06 g/m$^3$.

As a rough approximation one can distinguish four areas with different corrosive atmospheres: industrial, city, marine, and country air. Table 6.3 gives standard values of corrosion losses with regard to building metals in the open atmosphere. Figure 6.4 gives the corrosion

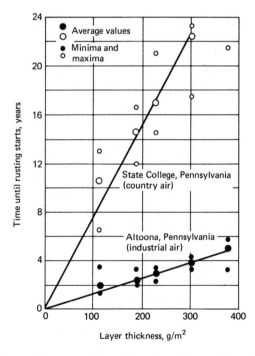

**Figure 6.4.** Life of zinc coated steel sheeting when weathered in relation to the thickness of zinc coatings.

losses per annum of galvanized steel sheeting in city and country air, respectively.

Rain favors corrosion by keeping metals moist and depositing impurities from the atmosphere onto the surface. However, rain also washes away corrosion inducing materials, and this may reduce the degree of corrosion. The $pH$ of slightly polluted rainwater is about 6. Close to industrial installations, rainwater $pH$ values as low as 3 (very acid) have been observed. The effects of these factors are roughly the same in closed and in covered spaces. Although there is no precipitation in enclosed areas, condensed water may lead to increased humidity (e.g., on water pipes). The relative air humidity in enclosed spaces often differs from that existing in the open air; in winter, for example, in heated rooms it is lower, while in summer it can be higher in cool cellars. On the whole the danger of corrosion in inside rooms is less than in the open air.

There are exceptions, of course, e.g., indoor swimming pools and waterworks (free chlorine), stables (ammonia), and chemical laboratories. Naturally, in every case where two different metals are connected so that an electric current may pass if moisture is present there is always a danger of corrosion (electrochemical corrosion).

Sections 6.1.2.2–6.1.2.6 give the properties of the most important building metals.

### 6.1.2.2 Aluminum

Aluminum is a metal with relatively low nobility, and therefore be expected to corrode rapidly. It weathers extremely well, however, because of the formation of a dense, firmly adherent, protective layer of aluminum oxide and hydroxide. The initial attack forms a reaction product which protects the surface against further corrosion. This protective layer, which is less than 0.1 micron in thickness, is rapidly renewed when the surface is damaged (i.e., it is self healing). It can be strengthened by anodic oxidation. With increasing purity the resistance against corrosion generally improves, but improvement can also be achieved by the addition of Mg, Si, and Mn as alloying components. In contrast, copper acts unfavorably. Industrial and maritime air, as well as strong chemical attack combined with frequent wetting, can cause increased corrosion of the surface. Voluminous corrosion products are formed, which roughen the surface and cause dirt to adhere. This thicker layer can protect against further corrosion if it is attached firmly, provided it is dried out repeatedly.

### 6.1.2.3 Lead

Lead is stable against the atmosphere, even when industrial pollutants are present. If exposed to $SO_2$ it forms a sparingly soluble protective layer of lead sulfate after oxidation; when it is exposed to sufficient $CO_2$ a protective layer of lead carbonate is formed.

### 6.1.2.4 Iron and steel

By far the most important atmospheric corrosion is the rusting of steel. It has enormous economic importance and is the reason why extensive measures of corrosion protection have had to be developed. Rusting of iron and steel is therefore described here in greater detail.

Appreciable corrosion only starts when the relative humidity of the air exceeds around 65%. In dry, pure air and below the freezing point of water there is no danger of corrosion. The formation of rust can best be described by the following equation:

$$2\,Fe + H_2O + 1\tfrac{1}{2}O_2 \longrightarrow 2FeO(OH)$$
$$\text{iron} + \text{water} + \text{oxygen} \longrightarrow \text{hydrated iron oxide}$$

Essentially, however, rusting is an electrochemical process, as has already been explained (sections 6.1.1.2.1 and 6.1.1.2.2 and Figures 6.2 and 6.3). Because of local differences of the electrochemical potential (e.g., rust/iron, carbon particles/iron, differences in structure) and the presence of an electrolyte (e.g., raindrops, tap water, salt solutions) an EMF is produced which amounts to a few hundred millivolts. This permits an electric current to flow. The EMF enables electrically charged particles (electrons and ions) to move, so that there is now a movement of both electricity and matter. Iron is dissolved from the metallic construction material and reacts with water and oxygen to form hydrated iron oxide. This reaction product is deposited as a spot of rust or, when the reaction has proceeded further, as a layer of rust. The rust layer is the sum of the reactions of numerous single corrosion cells. The impurities in the atmosphere, e.g., sulfur dioxide and chlorides, accelerate and complicate the corrosion process even at very low concentrations. This can be shown by the important example of $SO_2$.

Oxidation causes sulfur dioxide to form sulfuric acid in the presence of suitable catalysts:

$$SO_2 + \tfrac{1}{2}O_2 + H_2O \longrightarrow H_2SO_4$$

$H_2SO_4$ reacts with iron and oxygen to form ferrous sulfate and water:

$$Fe + H_2SO_4 + \tfrac{1}{2}O_2 \longrightarrow FeSO_4 + H_2O$$

The ferrous sulfate is then oxidized by oxygen to give ferric sulfate, which is then hydrolized to produce rust and sulfuric acid:

$$2\,FeSO_4 + \tfrac{1}{2}O_2 + 3H_2O \longrightarrow 2FeO(OH) + 2H_2SO_4$$

It should be noted that, in contrast to similar corrosion processes which take place with other building metals, the end product contains, apart from rust, more sulfuric acid. This can then dissolve more iron, and contributes to further rust formation. Sulfuric acid can therefore convert appreciable quantities of iron into rust in a continuous cycle. As with other building metals, it is possible for insoluble iron−sulfur compounds to be formed. Some of the sulfate may be removed from the cycle by separation or leaching out of the rust. Usually, however, the supply of new $SO_2$ and $SO_4^{2-}$ from the air predominates.

This sulfuric acid cycle during rusting is the reason why iron is the building metal most likely to be corroded by the external atmosphere. In addition, the layer of rust is porous and therefore permits other aggressive media to pass through. At best it can act as a corrosion retardant.

The composition of rust varies considerably. The following colors can be differentiated: orange, dark brownish red, black, green, and white rust. Orange rust consists of $FeO(OH)$.

Chromium−nickel steel and particularly chromium−nickel−molybdenum steels (e.g., 18% chrome, 10% nickel, 2−2.5% molybdenum) show good corrosion stability even under such aggressive atmospheric conditions as industrial and sea air, because they form oxidized protective layers. Pure chromium steel has poor corrosion resistance, but is suitable for interior use. Cast iron sometimes shows better corrosion resistance than steel, and this can be improved even further by the addition of more than 20% nickel.

Building steels with low phosphorus content (about 1%) and with additions of Cr, Cu, Ni, Mn, and Si (about .05% each) show increased corrosion resistance. They are described as being either weatherproofed or weather resistant. Although corrosion is not stopped altogether, it is reduced quite appreciably by the formation of dense and firmly adherent layers of rust. Such steels are particularly recommended for highly corrosive industrial atmospheres, which contain a good deal of sulfur dioxide, because sulfur dioxide aids the formation of a coating layer. In contrast, they are less suitable for use close to the coast or for constant contact with water and foundation structures. The layer of rust which produces this protective coating is probably sealed by sparingly soluble hydrated sulfates of copper and nickel. Chromium forms insoluble passive oxide layers. The formation of the coating layer takes between $1\frac{1}{2}$ and 3 years, depending on environmental conditions. While corrosion losses during the first 3 years amount to about $130 \, g/m^2$ year, they are only $10 \, g/m^2$ year later on, corresponding to an approximate reduction in thickness of 0.001 mm/year. During their development the color changes from light brown to brown and finally to brown-violet. When the layer is damaged, the process starts again and the protective layer is replaced.

As soluble iron compounds are produced especially at the beginning of the formation of the protective layers, it is possible for façade surfaces to exhibit rust patches. If appropriate preventive measures are taken during construction or correct building materials are chosen such unsightly phenomena can be reduced.

### 6.1.2.5  Copper

Copper is the most noble of the usual building metals and in consequence has extremely good resistance to atmospheric attack. The surface is coated initially with a protective dark brown to charcoal gray layer of copper oxide. This layer is converted over the years into a green patina. The patina is a mixture of copper hydroxide, copper carbonate, copper sulfate and copper chloride [$Cu(OH)_2$, $CuCO_3$, $CuSO_4$, $CuCl_2$], the proportions of which vary according to the composition of the surrounding air. The layer of patina adheres firmly to its base and is weather resistant. It is formed in marine air after about 4−6 years, in industrial and city air after about 5 years, and in country air after about 20−30 years. The protective patina layer is self healing. Copper alloys exhibit similar corrosion behavior to pure copper. Brass is, on the whole, somewhat less resistant, while tin bronze is somewhat better.

### 6.1.2.6   Zinc

The corrosion of zinc is closely related to the amount of $SO_2$ present, the relative humidity of the air, and, in coastal areas, also to the salt content of the air. Zinc is particularly stable in country air and in enclosed areas. A stable protective layer is formed, consisting of zinc oxide, zinc hydroxide, and zinc hydroxycarbonate [$Zn_2(OH)_2CO_3$]. This protective layer is self healing.

Appreciable disappearance of zinc takes place in city air (2−7 microns/year) and industrial air (3−22 microns/year). With average zinc coatings of 300−450 g/m$^2$ the protection against corrosion lasts for about 5−10 years in industrial air. The removal of zinc is caused by the $SO_2$ content of the air. $SO_2$ reacts with water to form sulfurous or sulfuric acid. These, in turn, react with the protective layer on the surface of the zinc, forming zinc sulfite or sulfate. The protective layer which is weakened in this way is then reformed by reaction of air with more metallic zinc. All this means that the zinc corrodes away. In marine air the annual removal of zinc amounts to about 1−7 microns, while close to the shore it is even higher.

Zinc corrodes particularly badly when it is exposed to condensation water. Such water can be formed on galvanized water pipes, underneath pipes, or underneath galvanized steel roofs because of humidity present in buildings. If this water cannot evaporate, white corrosion products are formed. If zinc is covered with condensed water for long periods of time and there is little or no access of carbon dioxide, it corrodes quite rapidly. The material can even be punctured by pitting.

Dipping galvanization in molten zinc enables thicker layers to be achieved than by electrolysis. Zinc applied by dipping, therefore, gives better protection against corrosion. The average durabilities of such coatings are given in Table 6.4.

Zinc can also be attacked by some materials used for the protection of timber and by bitumen, particularly blown bitumen. Impregnated timber roof joists must be separated by packing layers from galvanized sheet roofing. Bitumen attacks zinc because it forms acid reaction products under the action of ultraviolet rays. These acid products are then able to attack other building materials.

Galvanized steel sheets (assuming dense layers of zinc) and pure zinc sheets behave similarly under chemical attack. Titanium−zinc has been used for some years now for zinc sheeting. This is a zinc alloy with

**Table 6.4. Durability of Zinc Coatings as Corrosion Protection, years.** *(Source: van Eijnsbergen)*

| Atmosphere | Zinc Layer Thickness, $g/m^2*$ | | | |
|---|---|---|---|---|
| | 120 | 200 | 330 | 430 |
| Country air | 7 | 10 | 25 | 35 |
| Sea air | 6 | 8 | 15 | 25 |
| Industrial air | 2 | 4 | 7 | 9 |

*If the layer thickness in $g/m^2$ is divided by 7.13 (the density of zinc in $g/cm^3$) the average thickness in microns can be obtained.

0.12% titanium, 0.14-0.6% copper, and 0.01% aluminum. Such an alloy has improved mechanical properties, such as long term strength, ductility, etc.; in addition, its corrosion resistance to the atmosphere is much better because a protective layer containing titanium dioxide is formed.

Even damaged zinc coatings provide steel with some protection because of their unnoble character. Views differ regarding the distance over which such protection operates. When the damage which is incured is of the order of magnitude of pores only, protection is quite appreciable.

### 6.1.3 Corrosion in Aqueous Media

#### 6.1.3.1 General observations

It is more difficult to predict the corrosion properties of metals in aqueous media than in the atmosphere, mainly because aqueous media vary more extensively in composition, $p$H, temperature, conductivity, and degree of oxygenation than does the atmosphere. Apart from the formation of protective layers, electrochemical corrosion plays a more important part when aqueous media are involved.

Aluminum, lead, and zinc usually dissolve in acids and alkalis when the $p$H is less than 6 or more than 12. Iron is dissolved rapidly by acids under $p$H 4, more slowly up to $p$H 9, and not at all above $p$H 9.5. Copper is only dissolved by acids under oxidizing conditions.

Information regarding corrosion by given acids, alkalis, and salt solutions, by various industrial effluents, or within the chemical industry, is given in the literature references at the end of this book. In this text information is restricted to the cases of corrosion which occur most frequently in the building industry.

### 6.1.3.2   Rainwater and melted ice and snow

Rainwater is dealt with in section 6.1.2 above; the cases melted ice and snow are in the main similar to rainwater and condensation water (also dealt with in section 6.1.2).

### 6.1.3.3   Drinking water and consumption water

Tap water can be classified according to source into surface water and groundwater. Surface waters, e.g., rainwater and molten snow, contain very little salt i.e., they are soft. The same applies to groundwater which has been flowing through silicate rocks, such as granite, gneiss, or low lime mica. These waters contain varying quantities of dissolved oxygen and carbon dioxide. Groundwater frequently extracts salts from the soil in its path from the surface to reemergence. Water which contains particularly high concentrations of carbon dioxide dissolves calcium and magnesium carbonates to form the corresponding bicarbonates, which in their turn cause temporary bicarbonate hardness. Other salts, such as sulfates and nitrates, are also dissolved by water. The sum of the dissolved calcium and magnesium salts gives the total hardness. One can say in general that groundwaters are usually harder, but have less dissolved carbon dioxide and oxygen than surface waters. Tap water can therefore vary quite considerably in hardness and in oxygen and carbon dioxide contents. These three factors govern the corrosion processes in the affected installations, particularly pipelines. Additional factors are $pH$, velocity of flow, buffer capacity, and in some cases the presence of additional impurities.

Oxygen is usually the most corrosive component, particularly in the case of iron and copper. It not only oxidizes directly, but also accelerates electrochemical corrosion. Soft waters which contain oxygen and carbon dioxide are strongly corrosive. In addition, soft waters (containing less than about 3 milliequivalents/liter total hardness) which contain no oxygen or carbon dioxide also behave unfavorably since they do not cause formation of any protective layers. If the protective layer is thin or uneven, electrochemical cells (oxygen type) can form and cause corrosion. The formation of protective layers is disturbed by even very small quantities of chlorides, particularly in soft waters. The action of tap water upon various building materials is given below.

### 6.1.3.3.1  Aluminum

A protective layer of aluminum oxide and hydroxide is formed on aluminum products. Its stability depends upon $pH$, velocity of flow, and temperature of the water. Copper tends to induce corrosion (as little as 0.5 mg Cu/liter).

### 6.1.3.3.2  Lead

Lead is only resistant to waters which have an average or high degree of hardness (minimum hardness about 2.9 milliequivalents/liter) provided that they contain no carbonic acid. A protective layer of lead and calcium carbonate is formed. Soft waters and waters which contain carbonic acid do not permit this protective layer to be formed, but attack the surface. As dissolved lead solutions are poisonous, lead piping is totally unsuitable for the supply of drinking water.

### 6.1.3.3.3  Iron, steel, and zinc

Many waters have lime and carbonic acid in equilibrium. This is called equilibrium water, where there is sufficient carbon dioxide in solution to stabilize the carbonate. The equilibrium between dissolved calcium bicarbonate on the one hand, and free carbonic acid and sparingly soluble calcium carbonate on the other, can be expressed as follows:

$$CaCO_3 + H_2CO_3 \rightleftharpoons Ca(HCO_3)_2$$

Provided the minimum hardness is about 2.2 milliequivalents/liter, these waters form layers of mixed lime and rust that safeguard the steel piping against further corrosion. If the water contains an excess of carbonic acid, which prevents the formation of protective layers, there is a danger of corrosion of unprotected steel in the presence of oxygen.

In the case of zinc conditions are somewhat more favorable. When there is a certain excess of carbonic acid a protective layer of mixed zinc hydroxide and carbonate is formed. In addition, galvanized steel pipes offer electrochemical protection, in that during any corrosion the less noble zinc goes into solution first. With increasing temperature the rate of corrosion increases because the lime–carbonic acid equilibrium is shifted to the left, so that sparingly soluble calcium carbonate precipitates and the free carbonic acid content increases correspondingly. During subsequent cooling, e.g., by circulation in warm water and hot water appliances, equilibrium is not regained, but

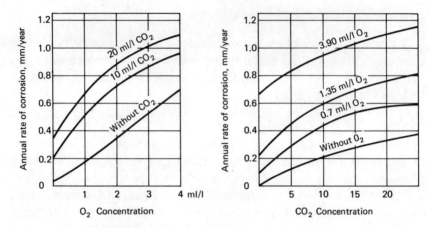

**Figure 6.5.** Corrosion behavior of high carbon steel (0.15%C) in water at 60°C as a function of oxygen and carbon dioxide contents.

an excess of carbonic acid remains. Corrosion can now occur. Figure 6.5 shows the corrosion properties of a carbon steel (0.15% C) in water at 60°C as a function of the oxygen and carbonic acid dissolved in the water.

Temperature plays an important role in zinc corrosion. As shown in Figure 6.6, zinc is strongly dissolved by distilled water at about 70°C.

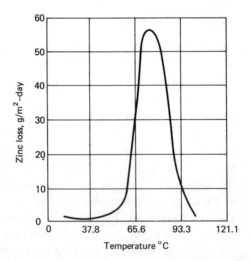

**Figure 6.6.** Velocity of dissolution of zinc in distilled and air saturated water as a function of water temperature. (Source: G. L. Cox)

The main reason for this is probably that the corrosion products produced within this temperature range are in the form of loose scales and do not adhere, in contrast to the situation at lower and higher temperatures, when strongly adherent protective layers are formed.

It should also be noted that a galvanized coating with its protective layer has a more noble character than iron at temperatures above about 70°C. In consequence, where the protective layer is damaged, the iron which lies underneath, and is now less noble, is subjected to pitting corrosion. It is possible for destructive attack to take place in this way. Zinc is suitable for warm water and hot water piping, where temperatures are above about 60°C, only under certain limited conditions. For cold water it is advisable to adapt the zinc coating to the nature of the water. A zinc layer of about 350 g/m$^2$ is sufficient for pipelines which carry water of average composition.

In heating plants with circulating water the oxygen originally present in the water is rapidly exhausted as protective layers are formed. After short periods of operation, the heated water is stripped of oxygen and, in consequence, there is no further danger of corrosion. If, however, oxygen is supplied too frequently, e.g., by changing or supplementing of the heating water when there are leaks, or when pumps are defective, corrosion damage can be expected. Oxygen is the main cause for corrosion, and other impurities in the water are of very slight consequence in comparison.

Traces of copper can cause pitting corrosion in steel and zinc piping when the protective layers are not very dense. For this reason copper pipelines should only be laid downstream of steel or galvanized steel piping. Cast iron piping and steel pipes lined with cement and mortar exhibit far better corrosion resistance.

*6.1.3.3.4 Copper*

Copper has proved to be a good construction material for cold and warm water piping. In normal cases the copper pipe is coated immediately with a thin layer of copper oxide, which changes later into basic copper carbonate and copper hydroxide chloride (patina). This only takes place if the water possesses at least average hardness, and oxygen is present.

Pitting corrosion can be noted particularly with cold water piping during the first three years of operation. This does not, however, occur very frequently. Soft water which contains free carbonic acid not only hinders the formation of a protective layer but can also cause direct corrosion. Irregular and perforated coating layers are bad, because they form anodic and cathodic sections. Chloride ions in water favor the formation of pitting corrosion. Their influence becomes appreciable when the concentration exceeds about 20 mg/liter. However, copper piping has been found to stay in good condition even with chloride concentrations in excess of 100 mg/liter. In addition, various other impurities, e.g., soldering flux or grains of rust, can induce pitting corrosion. Very high oxygen concentrations in the water, and internal stresses within the copper (e.g., due to cold forming) also favor corrosion. Clean and smooth copper surfaces offer the least opportunity for attack. Waters which contain ammonia and nitric acid attack copper.

Brass is somewhat more troublesome because of its tendency to "dezincification," contributed to by the presence of ions such as chlorides, especially when the zinc content is 15–30%. Nevertheless, the corrosion rate of brass is usually only between 0.07 and 0.7 mm/year.

### 6.1.3.4 River water

Pure river water is comparable to tap water. It can, however, have a degree of purity anywhere between that of drinking water and that of effluent water (Table 6.5). For this reason one cannot expect any uniform aggressive properties. Reference should be made to published literature, which shows that the aggressive properties depend on the type and concentration of impurities present. As as rough approxi-

**Table 6.5. Analytical Data on Water in Various German Rivers, 1967. (Source: Statistisches Jahrbuch der BRD)**

| River | Town | $Cl^-$, mg/liter | $SO_4^{2-}$, mg/liter | Oxygen Demand, mg/liter $KMnO_4$ | $Mg^{2+}$, mg/liter | Total Hardness, milliequivalents/ liter |
|---|---|---|---|---|---|---|
| Elbe | Geesthacht | 198 | 143 | 42 | | 6 |
| Weser | Veckerhagen | 1035 | 300 | 21 | | 12 |
| Rhine | Emmerich | 139 | 76 | 38 | 11 | 5 |
| Mosel | Koblenz | 165 | 80 | 23 | 15 | 7 |
| Danube | Jochstein | 15 | 24 | 18 | | 5 |

mation one may say that unalloyed steel corrodes in river water at an average rate of about 0.01 mm/year.

### 6.1.3.5 Seawater

Seawater has a high salt content, amounting to about 3.6% in the Atlantic and Pacific Oceans. Because of this, a fast rate of corrosive attack would be expected. Zinc gives good protection against corrosion because coating layers are formed on its surface by magnesium and calcium salts. Experiments by Hudson showed that a construction hot dipped in zinc with an average zinc coating layer of 900 g/m$^2$ showed no appreciable rust damage after 6 years of use in seawater. Similar observations were made with other zinc coated parts. An additional treatment with adherent paint coatings increases the lifetime of the structure quite appreciably.

Pure aluminum is attacked by seawater. There are, however, seawater resistant aluminum alloys (e.g., hydronalium, an alloy with Mg, Si, and Mn).

Seawater resistant copper alloys are copper-nickel-iron alloys, copper-zinc-aluminum alloys, and copper-zinc-tin alloys. Pure copper also has good resistance. According to La Que and Copson, the loss of corrosion is less than 0.02 mm/year.

Unalloyed steel, naturally, does not resist corrosion by seawater. A special "seawater rust" is formed which is actually very strongly corrosion inducing. One would expect corrosion rates of about 0.1 mm/year. But, for example, austenitic chromium-nickel-molybdenum steels resist seawater well. Although one cannot guarantee that no pitting corrosion will ever take place with austenitic chromium-nickel-molybdenum steels, chromium-nickel steels are certainly more likely to exhibit such damage.

Under long term action of seawater the iron in gray cast iron is dissolved out of the basic structure. The graphite framework which remains has little strength. Nickel-alloyed cast iron (15–30% nickel) behaves very much better, as can be seen from the figures given below (experimental conditions: nonaerated seawater at 50°C):

| Material | Loss, mm/year |
| --- | --- |
| unalloyed steel | 0.26 |
| unalloyed cast iron | 0.21 |
| nickel alloy cast iron | 0.12 |

### 6.1.4 Corrosion in Soil

#### 6.1.4.1  General Observations

A very large number of different factors affect corrosion in soil. Soils can be made up of a large number of different geological and chemical compounds. They can contain salts, acids and alkalis, as well as organic constituents. They may be extremely fine grained or very rough grained. The structure governs their porosity against air and moisture. Usually oxygen and water are required simultaneously for corrosion to occur, a condition which exists in many subsoils. The oxygen and carbonic acid concentrations, however, which are very important factors, may vary. Normally the oxygen content is lower and the carbon dioxide content higher than would be the case in air. Microorganisms and other factors are also important with respect to the aggressive action of soils.

#### 6.1.4.2  Factors Involved

##### 6.1.4.2.1  Types of Soil

When considering the typical soil components: sand, clay, chalk and humus, it is possible to establish the following triangular coordinate systems:

*humus free:* chalk–sand–clay
*clay free:* humus–chalk–sand
*sand free:* chalk–humus–clay
*chalk free:* sand–clay–humus

If these triangles are joined, a regular tetrahedron is obtained. Figure 6.7 shows these systems with the tetrahedron opened up. The shaded areas indicate likely aggressivity of the soil against metals. Because all the factors involved cannot be taken into consideration, only rough predictions are possible.

Sandy soils are usually only very slightly corrosive, because they contain hardly any corrosion inducing agents and easily drain off water. Clay soils aid corrosion, because they are impervious to water and have a very high moisture content, which promotes attack. If the soil is, however, completely saturated with water and contains no dissolved oxygen, no corrosion takes place, as long as there are no other corrosive materials (e.g., chlorides or sulfates) present.

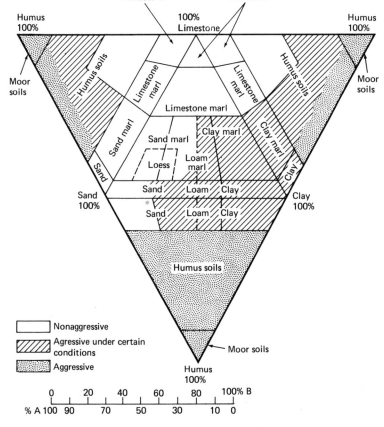

**Figure 6.7.** Survey of natural soils. (Source: Klas and Steinrath)

Chalk soils act as corrosion inhibitors because of their alkalinity, and because they are usually well drained. They hardly ever contain corrosion inducing substances.

Limestone deficient humus soils, moorland, and marshy soils cause strong corrosion, because they contain humic acid and other corrosive substances. They are usually very wet. Also, biological corrosion (see below) can contribute to corrosion in these soils. Artificial soils, e.g., soils made up of garbage and slag, as well as soils which are polluted with salts, fertilizers, and effluents, are usually very aggressive.

*6.1.4.2.2 Microorganisms*

Biological corrosion can cause considerable destruction of steel structures. The presence of the microorganism *Desulfovibrio desul-*

*furicans* is a case in point. These bacteria are found in clay soils or in soils in marshy and moorland areas. As oxygen is used up during oxidation of organic materials, these soils are virtually anaerobic. If they contain a high concentration of sulfates they then constitute a suitable environment for these microorganisms. Simply expressed, the corrosion process takes place as follows: reduce calcium sulfate to calcium sulfide, which reacts with carbon dioxide and water to form hydrogen sulfide; this hydrogen sulfide, and the sulfuric acid formed from it by an oxidation reaction which takes place when the soil dries out, corrode the iron.

### 6.1.4.2.3   Chemical and Physical-Chemical Factors

In order to find out just how aggressive a soil is, in addition to the type of soil involved, one also needs to know the following:

$p$H
Redox potential
Water content and dry matter content
Water holding capacity
Total acidity or total aklalinity
Percentage of carbon content
Results of physical examination of the soil, particularly the specific
    electric resistivity of the soil.
Qualitative and quantitative chemical analysis of the aqueous soil
    extract (particularly $Cl^-$, $SO_4^{2-}$, $S^{2-}$, and $CaCo_3/MgCo_3$)

Chlorides, sulfates, sulfides (which can be oxidized to sulfates), acid solutions, and humus are especially corrosive. The presence of chalk in the soil, which can neutralize acid components, inhibits corrosion.

Electrochemical cells can be formed on small metal surfaces in the soil, even if they only measure several square millimeters in area, although in such cases environmental conditions are reasonably uniform. Such uniform environmental conditions certainly do not exist with extensive pipeline networks. Different soils, varying permeabilities to air and water, varying moisture content, etc., all cause different diffusion velocities of oxidizing agents to the iron surface. This results in locally separated anodic and cathodic areas, i.e., macrocells. Rusting can then take place, mainly in the form of pitting corrosion.

Electrochemical cells are naturally also produced when two different metals are connected to each other in the soil in such a way that an electric current can pass. For example, if copper and steel pipes are laid next to each other and connected by means of metallic struts, the less noble steel piping corrodes.

The above criteria serve to classify the aggressivity of the soil. The specific resistivity of the soil is another very important factor. It can be measured fairly simply and governs the current passing in the macrocells. The electric resistivity depends upon the degree of dispersion of the solid components, which in its turn governs the permeability of the soils to air and water. As the dispersion changes from the colloid state to the macro state, the permeability increases. The specific soil resistivity measures the degree of aeration of a soil, and with it the chance of forming oxygen-type electrochemical cells (aerated cells).

Very thorough investigations were made by the U. S. National Bureau of Standards on steel piping sections with surfaces measuring a few hundred square centimeters. The values obtained are given in table 6.6. In assessing these values it should be noted that they were determined on relatively small samples. With increasing surface areas higher values are to be expected, depending on local conditions. According to Waters and co-workers, the relationship between specific and electric soil resistivity and corrosion behavior given in Table 6.7 can be expected for steel. When the electrical resistance of the soil is low, the electrochemical processes take place more efficiently. If different electrical resistances are found with soils in adjoining areas, it is likely that macrocells will be formed.

**Table 6.6.   Effects on Corrosion of Specific Resistivity of Soils.**
***(Source: National Bureau of Standards)***

| Specific Resistivity, ohm-cm | Limits of Pitting, mm/year | Average Depth of Pitting, mm/year |
|---|---|---|
| < 1,000 | 0.08−0.40 | 0.18 |
| 1,000−12,000 | 0.02−0.14 | 0.08 |
| > 12,000 | 0.015−0.12 | 0.03 |

**Table 6.7.   Conductivity of Soil, Resistivity of Soil and Expected Corrosion. *(Source: Waters et al.)***

| Specific Conductivity, cm/ohm | Specific Resistivity ohm/cm | Expected Corrosion Attack |
|---|---|---|
| $> 10^{-3}$ | $< 1,000$ | very strongly aggressive |
| $10^{-3} - 3.3 \times 10^{-4}$ | $1,000 - 3,000$ | strongly aggressive |
| $3.3 \times 10^{-4} - 2 \times 10^{-4}$ | $3,000 - 5,000$ | aggressive |
| $2 \times 10^{-4} - 10^{-4}$ | $5,000 - 10,000$ | moderately aggressive |
| $10^{-4} - 5 \times 10^{-5}$ | $10,000 - 20,000$ | slightly aggressive |
| $< 10^{-5}$ | $> 20,000$ | virtually nonaggressive |

### 6.1.4.3   Assessment of the Aggressivity of Soils

To determine the likelihood of corrosion, and to explain corrosion damage, the following observations, measurements and data should be correlated:

Visual examination of the soil in question.

Determination of specific electrical resistivity of the soil and, in certain cases, that of a complete soil profile.

*Extraction and Examination of Soil Samples*

To judge the aggressivity of soils to iron and steel (except high grade steel) the figures given in Table 6.8 can be used. They are determined from test results and collated. The qualitative assessment made from these data increases in reliability as the number of factors determined

**Table 6.8.   Coefficients Used for the Determination of Soil Aggressivity.**

| *1. Type of soil* | | |
|---|---|---|
| Limestone | | |
| Limestone marl | | $+2$ |
| Sand marl | | |
| Sand | | |
| Clay | | |
| Clay marl | | |
| Clay sand | Less than 25% colloidal | $0$ |
| Loam sand | | |
| Loam | | |
| Loam marl | | $-2$ |
| Humus | | |
| Peat | | |
| Slick | | $-4$ |
| Marshy soils | | |

*2. State of soil*
2.1 Air–water exchange zone aerated or unaerated—see 7.                            −2
2.2 Naturally developed soils.                                                      0
    Tipped soils.                                               −2
2.3 Uniform soil on building site.                                                  0
    Different soils on building site.                           −3

*3. Specific electric resistivity of soil measured by means of conductivity cell*
More than 12,000 ohm/cm                                                             0
Between 1000 and 12,000 ohm/cm                                                      −2
Less than 1000 ohm/cm                                                               −4

*4. Water content*
Less than 20%                                                                       0
More than 20%                                                                       −1

*5. pH*
$> 5$                                                                               0
$< 5$                                                                               −1

*6. Total acidity, up to pH 7*
$< 2.5$ milliequivalents/kg                                                         0
2.5–5.0 milliequivalents/kg                                                         −1
$> 5.0$ milliequivalents/kg                                                         −2

*7. Redox potential at pH 7*
$> 400$ millivolts (strongly aerated)                                               +2
200–400 millivolts (aerated)                                                        0
0–200 millivolts (slightly aerated)                                                 −2
$< 0$ millivolts (unaerated)                                                        −4

*8. Calcium and magnesium carbonate content, and total alkalinity up to pH 4.8*
$> 5\% = > 50,000$ mg/kg $= > 1000$ milliequivalents/kg                             +2
$1–5\% = 10,000–50,000$ mg/kg $= 200–1000$ milliequivalents/kg                      +1
$< 1\% = < 10,000$ mg/kg $= < 200$ milliequivalents/kg                              0

*9. Hydrogen sulfide and other sulfides*
Absent                                                                              0
Traces $= < 0.5$ mgS$^{2-}$/kg                                                      −2
Present $= > 0.5$ mgS$^{2-}$/kg                                                      −4

*10. Particles of coal or coke*
Absent                                                                              0
Present                                                                             −4

*11. Chloride ions*
$< 100$ mg/kg                                                                       0
$> 100$ mg/kg                                                                       −1

*12. Sulfate content*
$< 200$ mg/kg                                                                       0
200–500 mg/kg                                                                       −1
$> 500$ mg/kg                                                                       −2

*Note:* A coefficient has to be inserted separately for 2.1, 2.2 and 2.3.

**Table 6.9. Assessment of Soils by Means of the Coefficients Given in Table 6.8.**

| Sum of Coefficients | Assessment |
|---|---|
| $> 0$ | nonaggressive |
| $0-10$ | slightly aggressive |
| $< -10$ | strongly aggressive |

becomes larger (see Table 6.9). If only a few soil analyses have been carried out, these alone cannot give a reliable assessment of the behavior of pipeline networks. A large number of soil analysis results, even without measurement of the electrical soil resistance profile, can give some indication of the likelihood of corrosion. It is not yet possible to provide exact quantitative predictions regarding soil corrosion.

Everything which has been said up to now about soil corrosion applies to steel and cast iron, which are the most widely used materials. The data, however, can be applied to other metals as well. Zinc coating improves corrosion protection in soils, but it is advisable to employ a thicker layer of zinc than is normal for atmospheric corrosion protection: 450–600 g/m² against atmospheric corrosion, 900 g/m² and more against soil corrosion. According to van Eijnsbergen, zinc corrosion losses are much less than those of steel, but they are still quite appreciable (see Table 6.10). This means that in many soils, e.g., peat and marshland, zinc coating does not offer long term corrosion protection. On the other hand, zinc coated pipelines have remained undamaged in sandy soils for several decades.

Copper is more stable than zinc. As copper is also more noble than other building metals, care must be taken lest electrochemical cells be

**Table 6.10. Corrosion Losses from Mast Sockets in Finland. (Source: Van Eijnsbergen)**

| Soil | Steel Lost Ave., g/m²-year | Max., mm/year | Zinc Lost Ave., g/m²-year | Max., mm/year |
|---|---|---|---|---|
| Sand | 90 | 0.12 | 20 | 0.003 |
| Clay | 230 | 0.16 | 110 | 0.015 |
| Peat | 210 | 0.09 | 140 | 0.03 |

formed in the soil with other, less noble metals, because the latter would then corrode.

Lead can be attacked by calcium hydroxide, various chlorides, and humus. It can also be damaged by rats or by vibration stresses, although this is not usually considered to constitute corrosion.

### 6.1.4.4 Electrolytic or Galvanic Corrosion

A special case is electrolytic or galvanic corrosion, which causes considerable damage to installations laid into the soil. Stray direct currents cause electrolysis, e.g., in the vicinity of tramlines, trolley-bus lines, and electric lines, and electric trains. Corrosion of installations buried in the soil occurs at their anodic areas.

### 6.1.5 Corrosion by Nonmetallic Building Materials

Metallic building materials can be corroded by a large number of other building materials. Blown bitumen, for example, attacks zinc, while combustion gases originating from PVC form hydrochloric acid with moisture, which produces acid corrosion on steel and other metals. The most important corrosion of this type is the destruction of inorganic jointing materials such as cement, gypsum and magnesia mortar, and lime mortar.

Building lime and cement, as well as mortar and concrete made from these substances, are strongly alkaline. In the moist state they mainly attack aluminum and lead, but they also attack zinc. For this reason these metals have to be protected when being built into mortar and concrete by being painted with bitumen, synthetic resin lacquers, plastic laminates, etc. This applies particularly to aluminum and lead.

Gypsum and sulfate-containing magnesia cement can corrode iron and zinc strongly, with the formation of metallic sulfates. In these cases moisture is also a prerequisite.

Chlorides, which are found in magnesia cements, salt used to melt ice and snow, adhesives, and many other additives, attack building metals strongly, with the formation of metallic chlorides. It is possible for protective layers to be penetrated by such chlorides.

Slag can also attack metals, particularly iron and zinc, because it contains sulphur. If the building material is completely dry and no moisture comes into contact with it, no corrosion takes place.

## 6.2   CORROSION PROTECTION OF BUILDING METALS

### 6.2.1   General Observations

When corrosive media and building metals come into contact with each other, the following cases can occur:

1. *The metal is stable,* i.e., it is resistant to the corrosive medium (e.g., noble metals in air).
2. *The metal is passive,* i.e., it is protected by a natural protective layer, which has been formed prior to exposure to the corrosive medium (e.g., Ni–Mo steel in seawater).
3. *The metal is made passive,* i.e., when it is exposed to the corrosive medium a protective layer is formed which prevents futher corrosion (e.g., lead in sulfuric acid or iron in heavy metal phosphate solutions).
4. *The metal is totally unstable* in the corrosive medium.

In case 4 corrosion protective measures have to be taken. These protective measures are becoming of major importance, because of the rise in air pollution, increasing use of lightweight building techniques, and rising raw materials prices.

Corrosion protection should begin at the design and construction stage and corrosion inducing conditions must be avoided. For example, smooth and inclined areas are to be favored. In areas subjected to water spray the rate of attack is increased, and arrangements must be provided for good drying. The construction should be such that cleaning and painting is as easy as possible, i.e., good accessibility must be provided; in some cases special appliances for such work should be incorporated into the design. When piping is used in installations, it is best to employ either seam-free pipes, or welded pipes where the seams have been ground off, because such seams are liable to be affected by crevice and pitting corrosion. In the choice of construction materials due regard should be paid to any future liability to corrosion. With structures where access is difficult, it is necessary to use more corrosion resistant or better protected construction materials. When two metals are used together, they must be insulated from each other (Figure 6.8). In carrying out new building construction it is necessary to avoid damage to existing protective coatings. If damage

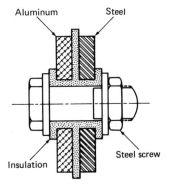

**Figure 6.8.** Ideal insulation of two metals.

does take place, it must be repaired immediately. For example, if a hot dip zinc coating is damaged it can be repaired by means of zinc paint. If all these points are observed subsequent corrosion protection is less expensive.

Corrosion prevention in the narrower sense can be classified as active or passive protection. In the case of active corrosion protection, either the materials itself or the corrosive medium is acted upon in such a way that no corrosion can take place. With passive corrosion protection, the exposure of the material to corrosive medium is prevented.

### 6.2.2 Active Corrosion Protection

*Influence of the Corrosive Medium*

The addition of suitable substances to prevent or reduce corrosion (inhibitors) to the corrosive medium can offer a certain degree of corrosion protection. Tapwater, for example, which contains aggressive carbon dioxide can best be treated at the water works, i.e., it can be neutralized with sodium hydroxide. If such central protective measures are not being carried out at the water works it is possible to install water preparation plants at decentralized locations, i.e., in the buildings themselves. Phosphates and silicates (which form protective layers), alkaline filter masses, and/or mechanical colloidal filters are used. Acid waters can also be neutralized or made weakly alkaline by the additon of sodium carbonate.

*Influence of the Construction Material*

Cathodic protection, which is the preferred method of rust prevention on iron and steel, is extremely important. It is assumed that the object which is being protected is in contact with an electrolyte (damp soil, seawater, etc.). The cathodic protection takes an active part in the electrochemical corrosion process. A protective current is produced which runs in the direction opposite to the corrosion current and possesses at least the same magnitude. The protective current supplies electrons to the metallic object which is to be protected. These react on the metal surface with ions of the reactive medium (oxygen, hydroxyl ions, etc.) and reduce them. An excess of electrons on the metal surface prevents the exit of positively charged metal ions from the object which is to be protected. In this way the protective current prevents the formation of a corrosion current and with it corrosion.

To produce the protective current one two methods can be used:

1. To protect objects which are limited in size in a well conducting environment (e.g., underground tanks, lock gates, ship hulls, etc.) it is preferable to use a galvanic (electrochemical) cell (Figure 6.9). A non-noble metal (usually magnesium or zinc: the anode) is connected electrically to the more noble object which one wishes to protect (usually steel: the cathode). Electrons flow from the anode via the insulated electric conductor to the cathode and corrosion is thereby prevented. Chemical changes, which always

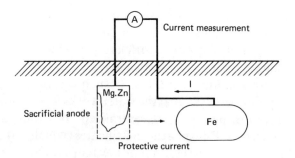

**Figure 6.9.** Cathodic protection of a buried container by means of a sacrificial anode.

take place with an electrochemical process, now proceed on the anode. This is gradually dissolved or corroded (positively charged magnesium or zinc ions enter the electrolyte). Because they gradually dissolve away, such devices are also called sacrificial anodes. They are usually dimensioned to last at least ten years. Depending on the size of the object, the electrical conductivity of the soil, etc., their mass is of the order of magnitude of several kg. For economic reasons and additional passive corrosion protection the object to be protected is also painted, so that the cathodic protection is only needed for places where the passive protection is defective.

2. For the protection of large objects it is preferable to carry out cathodic protection by means of a direct current using rectifiers fed from the main power line (Figure 6.10). This method permits higher current densities and more accurate adjustment of the protective current to the needs of the object. This method is used for the protection of pipelines laid in the ground. One single protective current appliance is sufficient for 30–40 km of pipeline length. For economic reasons, additional passive protection is also employed (e.g., a plastic mantle pipe). This considerably reduces the current demand and with it the maintenance cost. Considerable technical knowledge is required for the calculation and the construction of cathodic protection and special equipment is also needed. Work of this type should only be carried out by experienced specialized firms.

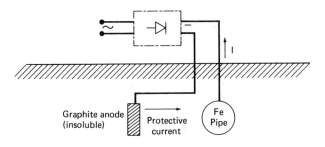

**Figure 6.10.** Cathodic protection of buried pipelines by means of applied current.

## 6.2.3   Passive Corrosion Protection

By far the most common corrosion protection layers that serve to separate the metal building component from corrosive media are metal coatings and organic coatings.

Nonmetallic inorganic coatings, such as vitreous enamel on sheet steel, or cement mortar encasing steel pipes, are rare. Zinc phosphate or zinc–iron phosphate layers (phosphating) on metallic surfaces. especially steel, are not used very often in the building industry. These phosphate layers alone do not constitute sufficient corrosion protection, and additional painting is necessary. Phosphate coatings are commonly used for steel pretreatment in the automobile industry.

### 6.2.3.1   Metallic Coatings

The following methods for the application of such coatings are used:

1. Electrolysis (e.g., galvanic nickel plating)
2. Dipping into molten metals (e.g., hot-dip zinc coating)
3. Diffusion (e.g., diffusion chromium plating)
4. Spraying of liquid metals (e.g., zinc coating by spraying)
5. Rolling thin foils onto the surfaces (e.g., gold leafing)

Before coatings are applied, the metal surfaces must be cleaned carefully both mechanically and chemically. Surfaces must be degreased and pickled.

#### 6.2.3.1.1   Electrodeposition, Galvanizing

To produce galvanic metal coatings, electrolysis is employed. The metal which is to be coated serves as the cathode while the metal which constitutes the coating is the anode. A salt solution of the metal used for coating is employed as electrolyte (electrolysis bath). The cations of the electrolyte, which is the metal coating, migrate to the cathode, or the metal to be coated, and precipitate. The anode is gradually dissolved and in this way supplies metal ions to the electrolyte and to the protecting layer. In practice, numerous details, such as concentration, composition and temperature of the electrolyte, must be carefully controlled, or dense and well adherent protective layers will not form. To improve adhesion, intermediate layers of other metals are often galvanized on, as for example, copper on iron underneath nickel.

Electrolysis is also used for strengthening the protective oxide layer in the case of aluminum. The aluminum is connected as the anode and oxidized anodically during the process of electrolysis. This anodizing is also called the Eloxal technique in Germany. Such an oxide layer, which is many times thicker than natural surface oxidation, is hard and can be made transparent, opaque, or colored. Apart from the thickness of the layer, its density, which is governed by the way it is made, has an appreciable influence on its protective action.

### 6.2.3.1.2  Dipping in Molten Metals

Hot-dip coatings are formed by immersion in molten metals. Zinc coating, which proceeds at about 450°C, is of particular importance. When steel is dipped into zinc, a zinc–iron alloy is formed on the steel surface which is topped by a layer of pure zinc. Zinc coatings amounting up to 400–900 g/m$^2$ are common nowadays for steel structures exposed to the atmosphere. Surface defects and other imperfections of such zinc coated steel can be covered over by spray application or by means of a paint which contains zinc dust.

In many cases hot-dip zinc coatings of this type provide adequate protection against corrosion. In other cases, it is advisable or necessary to apply additional paint coatings. In an aggressive atmosphere or in aggressive soils the protective action is drastically increased when hot-dip zinc coating application is combined with painting. Such protection lasts $1\frac{1}{2}$–$2\frac{1}{2}$ times as long as the sum of the durations of each protective action alone. The reason for this is that creeping corrosion underneath paint films is prevented. Paint can be applied at the galvanizing plant on the freshly deposited zinc surface. Typical paints used are chlorinated latex, modified alkyd resins pigmented with calcium orthoplumbate, epoxy-phenolic resin compounds for stoving lacquers, etc. It is also possible to apply paints later on some weathered surfaces. Such paint coatings are epoxy resins with polyamide hardeners, two part polyurethane resins, and acrylate resins with isocyanate hardener.

### 6.2.3.1.3  Diffusion Treatment

This process is called cementation. For the production of chromium coatings, for example, the metal parts are heated in an autoclave with chromium salts. Chromium goes into the gaseous phase and can then diffuse into the boundary layer of the metal surface. An insoluble chromium-containing phase is produced with decreasing chromium content from outside to inside. The chromium content should usually be at least 12% at a depth of 0.1 mm. Corrosion resistance is roughly the same as that of stainless chromium steel, but production costs are lower.

#### 6.2.3.1.4 Sprayed Metal Coatings

Metals which melt easily, such as zinc and aluminum, etc., are sprayed onto the metal surface in atomized form by means of special pistol shaped appliances, and solidify in the form of adherent scales. Metal coatings which have been applied by this technique are usually very porous, and therefore almost always require additional painting.

### 6.2.3.2 Organic Coatings

#### 6.2.3.2.1 General Observations

Such surface coatings as paints, varnishes, and similar materials consist of a medium (e.g., linseed oil or chlorinated latex), a pigment (e.g., red lead or iron oxide), and usually solvents (e.g., white spirits and naptha). The following conditions must be fulfilled for the paint coating to have a long life:

1. The surface to be protected must be in good shape.
2. The minimum thickness of the paint film must accord with specifications.
3. The correct paints must be chosen for the job at hand.
4. The paint must be applied correctly.

If any one of these requirements is not fulfilled the life expectancy of the paint film, which can amount to 15–20 years when the paint is applied properly, is very much reduced.

The distinction between painting and coating layer application is not clearly defined. The main criterion for paints is that they can be applied by simpler methods (e.g. brush application) which produces thin films. To obtain an adequate protective coating it is necessary to build up several layers. Coating layer application, on the other hand produces thick layers in very few working stages but takes time to apply. Spatula spreading is a good example.

As the main use for organic coatings is for structural steel, this subject is dealt with in greater detail. Tables 6.11 and 6.12 describe

## Table 6.11.  Classes of Corrosion Protection as Given in DIN 4115.

| Use of Lightweight Steel Components | Accessibility After Assembly[1] | Necessary Corrosion Protection Class |
|---|---|---|
| Inside closed rooms with normal corrosion conditions. Also in open air and non-enclosed spaces in country air with low aggressivity | accessible<br><br>not accessible | K3<br><br>K2 |
| In the open air and non-enclosed spaces with normal industrial atmosphere with average aggressivity (city air) | accessible<br><br>not accessible | K2<br><br>K1 |
| In cases of abnormally bad corrosion conditions. Examples are: Heavy industrial atmospheres, marine atmospheres or inside chemical factories | accessible | corrosion protection depends on conditions minimum = K1 |
| | Not accessible sections, apart from hollow profiles, are not permissible | |

[1]In this context, "accessible" means that steel building components can be inspected and new surface protection applied without excessive work having to be done. If this is not the case the components are "not accessible."

## Table 6.12.  Corrosion Protection Systems as Given in DIN 4115.

| Corrosion Protection Class | Protective Measures | |
|---|---|---|
| | Surface Pretreatment | System of Protection |
| K1 | Ready for zinc coating. | Zinc coated by dipping. Protective layer at least 50 microns thick, equivalent to 350 g/m² of surface. Two to three strongly adherent paint films.[1] |
| | | Zinc coated by dipping. Protective layer at least 80 microns thick, equivalent to 560 g/m² of surface. Two strongly adherent paint films.[1] (Steel thicknesses in excess of 3 mm.) |
| | | Zinc coated by dipping. Protective layer at least 25 microns thick, equivalent to 175 g/m² of surface. Strongly adherent, dense protective coating of plastic applied at the factory. |

## Table 6.12 (continued)

| | | |
|---|---|---|
| | Sandblasting[2] to shiny metal surface or equivalent chemical rust removal in an acid vat. | Sprayed zinc coating or aluminum coating. Layer thickness at least 100 microns. Two strongly adherent paint coatings.[1] |
| | | Double layer of lead coatings. One layer to be applied by dipping and the other by electrolysis. Layer thickness at least 200 microns. In some cases the surface is also painted with, for example, chlorinated latex paint. |
| | | Plastic coating applied by powder sintering technique (either by turbulent flow method or electrostatic method). Layer thickness at least 200 microns. |
| | | Three coatings of two-part epoxy resin or two-part polyurethane, or two coatings of tar pitch–epoxy resin. Total thickness at least 300 microns. |
| K2 | Ready for zinc coating. | Zinc coated by dipping. Protective layer at least 25 microns thick, equivalent to 175 g/m[2] of surface. Two strongly adherent paint coatings,[1] or dense plastic coating layer. |
| | Sandblasting[2] to shiny metal surface or equivalent rust removal in an acid vat. | Sprayed zinc coating or aluminum coating. Layer thickness at least 50 microns. Two strongly adherent paint coatings.[1] |
| | | Plastic coating applied by powder sintering technique (either by turbulent flow method or electrostatic method). Layer thickness at least 200 microns. |
| | | Two coatings of two-part epoxy resin or coal tar pitch–epoxy resin. Total thickness at least 150 microns. |
| | Sandblasting to shiny metal surface.[2] Removal of rolling scale skin and sandblasting to shiny metal surface (derusting grade 3) when using paint incorporating zinc powder. | Two priming layers of red lead, zinc chromate, or powdered zinc paint, together with two top coats of iron oxide paint. Total thickness at least 130 microns. One priming layer and two to three layers of paint made from either coal tar pitch, petroleum pitch, or a combination of the two with fillers. Total thickness at least 250 microns. |

| K3 | Sandblasting to shiny metal surface.[2] Removal of rolling scale skin and sandblasting to shiny metal surface (derusting grade 3) when using paint incorporating zinc powder. | One or two priming layers of red lead, zinc chromate, or powdered zinc paint, together with one top coat of iron oxide paint. Total thickness between 70 and 100 microns. One priming layer and two coats of paint made from coal tar pitch, petroleum pitch, or a combination of the two, with fillers. Total thickness at least 150 microns. |

[1]Very thin priming coats applied to improve adhesion do not count as paint coats in this context.
[2]Sandblasting is not recommended with steel thicknesses less than 3 mm because the material may be distorted.

three corrosion protection classes for various uses, and recommend the appropriate protective systems.

### 6.2.3.2.2 Surface pretreatment

Foreign matter such as dust, grease, oil, etc.; as well as any loose bits of the material itself, have to be removed before the paint is applied. It is necessary that the surface to be treated is absolutely clean, and to remove any traces of rust.

Mechanical methods (e.g., wire brush), thermal methods (e.g., torch), and chemical techniques (e.g., acid treatment) can all be used. Sand blasting is the most important method. In this connection it should be noted that while the surface roughness, produced by sand blasting aids adhesion, it is necessary that the undercoat that follows covers all such imperfections. In practice, an average roughness depth of about 70 microns has been found to be suitable. Under normal working conditions it can be achieved with a quartz/sand mixture with grain sizes between about 0.5 and 1.2 mm. The following standards of rust removal are employed:

1. Cleaning and removal of surface rust. Firmly adherent paint film is left undisturbed.
2. Cloudy metal surface remains after rust removal.
3. Shiny metal surface remains which is completely free from rust, paint, and rolling scale.

It is usually only possible to achieve the first degree of rust removal using manual methods. Flame treatment can provide degrees 1 and 2, while sandblasting can achieve 1, 2, and 3.

The degree of rust removal required depends mainly on the type of paint to be applied and the expected degree of corrosion loading (table 6.13). Durability is increased when the surface is treated more thoroughly.

Rust converting substances can change rust into stable and firmly adherent compounds and in this way provide a suitable surface for paint films. When such materials are used (e.g., mixes based on phosphoric acid) a firmly adherent and stable iron compound (e.g., phosphate) is formed. A difficulty which arises is that when too little phosphoric acid is used, rust remains, while when too much phosphoric acid is used, the iron itself can be attacked. In both cases the corrosion process continues further. For this reason many authorities disapprove of rust converting substances.

After the rust removal process has been completed the first paint film must be applied immediately; this is an adherent primer. So-called wash primers increase the adhesion to steel and zinc. At the same time they avoid the danger of creeping corrosion underneath the paint film.

*6.2.3.2.3 Nature and application of paint coatings*

Corrosion protective paint coatings have to fulfill two tasks:

1. They must constitute a protective and passive film on the surface of the material.
2. They must be resistant against external agents.

To achieve this, a completely pore-free coating is necessary; this requires a minimum layer thickness. The coating can usually be made pore-free and sufficiently thick only by using several coats. The following minimum layer thicknesses serve as standard values for different exposure conditions:

*Country air:* 125 microns
*City air:* 180 microns
*Industrial air:* 300 microns
*Sea air:* 250 microns

The minimum number of coats needed to achieve the required layer thickness, depends on the paint vehicle. The average dry layer thickness of single paint films for various vehicles are as follows:

*Vinyl resin:* 10–20 microns

*Chlorinated hydrocarbon:* 15–25 microns
*Polycyclic latex:* 15–25 microns
*Alkyd resin:* 25–30 microns
*Oil:* 35–40 microns

Specially formulated paints can be used to obtain thicker single layers without degradation of performance. These thick layer paint coatings have appreciable economic advantages.

A multilayer buildup allows each layer to have a different purpose. The primer, which is applied directly upon the metal surface, should have good adhesion and protect well against corrosion. Suitable pigments help to achieve this (see section 6.2.3.2.4 below.) In addition, the primer should cover any imperfections in the surface. The top coat has to protect the priming coat against destruction and erosion, i.e., it must be stable against environmental action. This is also the function of the paint vehicle in combination with pigments and fillers.

In the case of objects which are not exposed to particularly drastic conditions, four coats (two undercoats and two top coats) are usual. In industrial atmospheres up to six coats are not rare. When thick coating systems are used, providing dry layer thicknesses of up to 150 microns per working stage, fewer coats are needed.

It is important that edges, rivets, screws, etc., be adequately covered, as paint lacks adhesion or forms thin layers at such positions, so that these sections are particularly liable to corrode. To avoid such weak zones an additional coating with a paint putty should be applied on such parts between the primer and the top coat. It is best if the putty is a different color to facilitate checking whether all weaknesses have been covered in this way.

The best technique of painting is still brush application. In a brush application system the different coats should have different colors so that they can be distinguished for control purposes.

The various paints must be thoroughly stirred prior to application, and may only be applied on a completely dry and clean surface. As even the smallest quantity of moisture interferes, painting should be avoided when the relative humidity of the air is in excess of 80% or below 5%.

Complete drying or hardening of all paints except hot-dip applied coats requires a certain curing time, during which the solvent evaporates, polymerization proceeds, etc. Only after this time has passed does the paint film achieve its maximum protective effect.

Corrosion loading should, as far as possible, start only after curing. This precaution increases the lifespan of the paint film.

*6.2.3.2.4 Paint materials*

The numerous types of paints on the market can be classified by the following characteristics:

1. *Composition*
   1.1. Vehicle (oil, synthetic resin, bitumen, etc.)
   1.2. Pigments (red lead, iron oxide, zinc powder, etc.)
2. *Drying and hardening*
   Air drying, thermosetting, catalytic setting, reaction with metals.
3. *Application technique*
   Brushing of lacquers, spatula (knife) application of pastes, stoving lacquers, etc.
4. *Purpose*
   Rust protective coatings, sealers, chemical resistant coatings, etc.

Oils, plastics, and bituminous substances are all used as vehicles. Pigments are subdivided into active and passive types. The task of active pigments is usually to protect iron by passivation, which is the formation of a thin, firmly adherent oxide skin. Typical pigments of this type are red lead, lead powder, calcium plumbate, zinc powder, and zinc chromate. Active pigments, such as oxides of iron, protect because of their flake-like structure, which provides dense packing and with it good protective action.

The properties of the widely used red lead–linseed oil paint deserve fuller mention. As steel surfaces are never completely free from oxides, and therefore anodic and cathodic areas are always present, moisture and oxygen causes corrosion on the boundary area between metal and paint. The reactions which take place (Figure 6.11) are roughly as follows. Hydrogen produced in the cathodic area (iron oxide) is oxidized by the red lead to water, and the red lead itself is reduced to plumbous oxide. This plumbous oxide forms a corrosion retarding coating. The iron ions which are liberated in the anodic area react with the hydroxyl ions produced at the cathode to form ferrous hydroxide. Red lead oxidizes this ferrous hydroxide, and is reduced in consequence. Both reaction products are produced as an intimate mix and

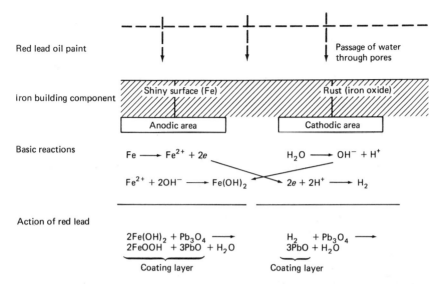

**Figure 6.11.** Corrosion protection by means of red lead paint. (Source: Henning-Knöfel)

constitute a dense, corrosion retarding and passive coating. The plumbous oxide reacts with the linseed oil to form lead soaps. Ions which penetrate the coating are made harmless by reaction with lead and hydroxyl ions. Because red lead has both an oxidizing and a passivating action no creeping corrosion can take place, even if the paint coat is scratched.

A list of vehicles and pigments frequently used for corrosion protection follows. Various vehicles and pigments are commonly mixed in paint formulations.

*Media*
   a. *Against atmospheric corrosion:* linseed oil, oil–alkyd resin, bituminous materials.
   b. *Against chemical corrosion:* chlorinated hydrocarbons, polycyclic latex, epoxy resin, polyethylene, polychloroprene, polyester, polyurethane, vinyl resin.

*Pigments*
   a. *Against atmospheric corrosion:* aluminum, red lead, white lead, calcium plumbate, iron oxide, titanium dioxide, zinc chromate, zinc oxide, zinc powder.

b. *Against chemical corrosion:* lead powder, iron oxide, graphite, silicon carbide, titanium dioxide, zinc oxide.

The following criteria apply in choosing of paints to be used:

1. Best possible stability in the conditions expected.
2. Minimum labor costs.
3. Minimum raw-material costs.

Criterion 1 refers mainly to weather resistance (to dampness, ultraviolet light, condensation water, industrial flue gases, etc.), chemical resistance (to acids, alkalis, salts, oils, etc.), mechanical resistance (to abrasion, vibration, impact, etc.), thermal resistance, and similar factors. It should also be borne in mind that it is not possible to apply every kind of paint to every kind of surface. (See Tables 6.13 and 6.14).

With regard to criterion 2, it is necessary to consider such factors as drying time, ventilation requirements, temperature and environmental effects, applicability of thick layer systems, surface requirements, and ease of repair of paint films.

With regard to criterion 3, it is necessary to consider not only the actual cost of the paint but also the life expectancy of the paint layer.

As can be seen, there can be no universal paint which satisfies all the requirements.

Oil paints protect well against atmospheric corrosion, but tend to swell when strongly wetted. Bituminous paints behave better under such conditions. Paints based on coal tar have fungicidal and bactericidal properties. When the environmental conditions are more aggressive than this, it is best to choose paints made from synthetic resins. Properties of such paints are given in Tables 6.15 and 6.16. It is advisable to consult established paint manufacturers regarding suitable paints for specific uses.

Paint coatings on zinc surfaces were discussed in section 6.2.3.1.2. It is advisable to apply paint to aluminum surfaces, particularly in industrial air and sea air. When properly applied these exhibit a long life expectancy, as creeping corrosion cannot take place. Thorough pretreatment of the metal surface is a prerequisite for long durability. The metal must be cleaned mechanically, degreased, and perhaps acid treated. It is usual to continue with a wash primer, which reacts with the metal to provide a firm foundation. A primer based on zinc chromate is then applied and two top coats of paints free from lead and

**Table 6.13. Relationship Between the Paint Used and the Degree of Rust Removal Needed.**

| Types of Paints | Degree of Rust Removal | | |
|---|---|---|---|
| | 1 | 2 | 3 |
| *Pigments* | | | |
| Red lead | 0 | + | + |
| Lead powder | − | − | + |
| Calcium plumbate | − | + | + |
| Zinc chromate | − | + | + |
| Zinc powder | − | − | + |
| *Paint media* | | | |
| Bitumen | 0 | + | + |
| Alkyd resin | 0 | + | + |
| Petroleum pitch | 0 | + | + |
| Chlorobutadiene | − | − | + |
| Chlorinated latex and media containing chlorinated latex | 0 | + | + |
| Chlorosulfonic polyethylene | − | − | + |
| Cyclized latex and media containing cyclized latex | 0 | + | + |
| Epoxy resin | − | + | + |
| Oil | − | + | + |
| Modified oil media | 0 | + | + |
| Modified bituminous media | 0 | + | + |
| Polyurethane | − | + | + |
| Coal tar pitches | 0 | + | + |
| Styrene−butadiene | − | − | + |
| Unsaturated polyesters | − | + | + |
| Vinyl resins | 0 | + | + |
| Media made from setting materials and bituminous substances | − | + | + |
| Silicone−alkyd resins | − | − | + |
| Silicone resin | − | − | + |

*Symbols:* + sufficient, 0 sufficient under certain conditions, − insufficient

copper are brushed on (e.g., alkyd resin, polyurethane resin, or acrylic resin types.)

Bituminous paints are also used, and in such a case priming with paints that can react with metals improves adhesion. A combination of bitumen with epoxy resin has been found to be of value. For heavy duty use underneath water, materials such as chlorinated rubber, polyvinylchloride, and two-part varnishes based on epoxy resin or polyurethane are suitable.

Table 6.14.   Paints and How They Can Be Used on Different Surfaces. (Source: Wesche)

| Type of Medium | Plasters | Normal Concrete | Facing Concrete | Brickwork Walls | Other Stone Walls | Asbestos Cement | European Timber | Tropical Timber | Steel and Iron | Aluminum Alloys | Zinc |
|---|---|---|---|---|---|---|---|---|---|---|---|
| | O  I | O  I | O  I | O  I | O  I | O  I | O  I | O  I | O  I | O  I | O  I |
| **AQUEOUS MEDIA** | | | | | | | | | | | |
| Distempers | + + | + + | − − | + + | + + | − − | − − | − − | − − | − − | − − |
| White cement mixed with dispersions | + + | + + | + + | + + | + + | + + | − − | − − | − − | − − | + + |
| Colored waterglass | + + | + + | + + | + + | + + | + + | − / | − − | − − | + + | + + |
| **Glues and adhesives** | | | | | | | | | | | |
| Hide and bone glue | − + | − + | − + | − + | − + | − − | − − | − − | − − | − − | − − |
| Alginates (Irish moss) | − + | − + | − + | − + | − + | − − | − − | − − | − − | − − | − − |
| Starch adhesives | − + | − + | − − | − + | − + | − − | − − | − − | − − | − − | − − |
| Methylcellulose | − + | − + | − − | − + | − + | − − | − − | − − | − − | − − | − − |
| Cellulose glycollate | − + | − + | − / | − + | − + | − − | − − | / | − − | − − | − − |
| Starch–ether | − + | − + | − − | − + | − + | − − | − / | / | − − | − − | − − |
| Casein glues | − + | − + | − − | + + | + + | − − | − / | / | − − | − − | − − |
| Casein–lime | + + | + + | − / | + + | + + | + + | − − | − / | − − | − − | − − |
| **Emulsions and dispersions** | | | | | | | | | | | |
| Casein–oil emulsions | + + | + + | + + | + + | + + | + + | + + | / | − − | + + | + + |
| Alkyd emulsions (oil–water type) | + + | + + | + + | + + | + + | + + | + + | / | − − | + − | + + |
| Alkyd emulsions (water–oil type) | + + | + + | + + | + + | + + | + + | + + | / | + − | + + | + + |
| Polyvinyl acetate dispersions | + + | + + | + + | + + | + + | + + | + + | / | − − | + + | + + |
| Polyvinyl acetate copolymer dispersions, either alone or mixed with lime or cement | + + | + + | + + | + + | + + | + + | + / | / | − − | + / | + / |
| Polystyrene dispersions and similar materials | + + | + + | + + | + + | + + | + + | + + | / | − − | − − | − − |
| Polyvinyl propionate dispersions | + + | + + | + + | + + | + + | + + | + + | / + | − − | + + | + + |
| Synthetic rubber latex | + + | + + | + + | + + | + + | + + | + − | / | − − | + − | + + |
| **OIL AND VARNISH MEDIA** | | | | | | | | | | | |
| Linseed oil varnish | + + | + + | + + | + + | + + | + + | + + | / | + + | + + | + + |
| Linseed oil and China wood oil (or tung oil) stand oils | + + | + + | + + | + + | + + | + + | + + | / | + + | + + | + + |
| Blown linseed oil | + + | + + | + + | + + | + + | + + | + + | / | + − | + + | + + |

| Coating | | | | | | | | | | | | | | | | | |
|---|---|---|---|---|---|---|---|---|---|---|---|---|---|---|---|---|---|
| **Oil varnishes** | | | | | | | | | | | | | | | | | |
| Stand oil–enamel lacquers | + | + | + | + | + | + | + | + | + | + | + | + | + | + | + | + | + |
| Oil–resin varnishes, either colorless or pigmented | + | + | + | + | + | + | + | + | + | + | + | + | + | + | + | + | + |
| Alkyd resin varnishes with added oil | + | + | + | + | + | + | + | + | + | + | + | + | + | + | + | + | + |
| Quick drying alkyd resin varnishes | + | + | + | + | + | + | + | + | + | + | + | + | + | + | + | + | + |
| **Two-part varnishes** | | | | | | | | | | | | | | | | | | |
| Polyurethane varnishes | + | + | + | + | + | + | + | + | + | + | + | + | + | + | + | + | + |
| Amino hardened epoxy resin varnishes | + | + | + | + | + | + | + | + | + | + | + | + | + | + | + | + | + |
| Acid hardened setting varnishes | – | – | – | – | – | – | – | / | – | – | – | – | / | – | / | – | + |
| **Stoving varnishes** | | | | | | | | | | | | | | | | | | |
| Alkyd resin–amino resin copolymer baked at 80°C, for the auto industry. | – | – | – | – | – | – | – | – | – | – | – | – | – | – | + | + | + |
| Alkyd resin–amino resin copolymer baked at 120°C for general industry | – | – | – | – | + | + | – | – | + | + | + | + | + | + | + | + | + |
| **Oil-free varnishes (drying by evaporation only)** | | | | | | | | | | | | | | | | | | |
| Spirit varnishes (made from shellac and other resins soluble in methylated spirits) | – | – | – | + | + | + | + | + | + | – | – | + | + | + | + | + | + |
| Nitrocellulose–Zapon lacquers | – | – | – | + | + | + | + | + | – | – | – | + | + | + | – | + | + |
| Pigmented nitrocellulose lacquers | – | – | – | + | + | + | + | – | – | / | + | + | + | – | + | + | + |
| Matte nitrocellulose finishes | – | – | / | – | / | + | – | – | – | – | + | + | + | + | – | + | + |
| Vinyl resin copolymer lacquers | + | / | + | + | + | + | + | + | + | + | + | + | + | + | + | + | + |
| Wash primer made from acetal resin medium | – | – | + | + | + | / | – | + | + | / | + | + | + | + | + | / | + |
| **Rubber derivatives** | | | | | | | | | | | | | | | | | | |
| Chlorinated latex varnishes | + | + | + | + | + | + | + | + | + | + | + | + | + | + | + | + | + |
| Cyclized latex varnishes | + | + | + | + | + | + | + | + | + | + | + | + | + | + | + | + | + |
| **Specialized finishes** | | | | | | | | | | | | | | | | | | |
| Unsaturated polyester varnishes | / | / | + | + | + | + | / | / | / | / | + | + | + | + | + | – | – |
| Polyethers and polyesters combined with diisocyanates | / | / | + | + | + | + | / | / | / | / | + | + | + | + | + | – | – |

*Symbols:*  O = outside use    I = inside use  
+ = good    / = can be used    – = unsuitable

## Table 6.15. Properties of Synthetic Resin Paints—One Part Coatings. *(Source: Wesche)*

*Type of medium*  Alkyd resins

*Fundamentals*  Alkyd resin paints are related to oil paints; they are produced by esterification of polyvalent alcohols (for example glycerol and glycols) with various organic acids such as phthallic acid. Alkyd resins are usually modified by condensing with natural drying and non-drying oils.

*Paint properties*  Good weather resistance, average stability against chemicals, water, heat (about +120°C), and abrasion; dries rapidly, has high degree of gloss and smooth surface.

*Advantages*  Excellent water, chemical, and heat resistance in comparison to oil paints, without any reduction of weather resistance; dries more quickly, higher degree of gloss and surface smoothness.

*Disadvantages*  There may be adhesion difficulties if not correctly formulated, when painting sandblasted surfaces on which tiny rust particles have already been reformed, or on surfaces which are slightly moist.

*Uses*  Steel structures such as large halls, cranes, and bridges.

---

*Type of medium*  Chlorinated rubber

*Fundamentals*  There are three different basic types of chlorinated rubber media:
  a. Clorinated rubber with plasticiser as the medium itself.
  b. Chlorinated rubber in combination with other media (e.g., alkyd resin).
  c. Chlorinated rubber as a minor constituent of oil paints.

*Paint properties*
  *a. Chlorinated rubber:*  Paints with good resistance to mineral oil, fats, chemicals, and water; nonflammable, satisfactory weather resistance, relatively high surface hardness.
  *b. Chlorinated rubber–alkyd resin:*  Paints which do not have to satisfy very strict specifications regarding chemical resistance and surface hardness.
  c. Clorinated rubber addition to oil paints gives faster touch drying and hard drying, better hardness, and some resistance to chemicals.

*Advantages*  Fairly simple paints with wide range of uses.

*Disadvantages*
  *a. Chlorinated rubber:*  Poor dry layer thickness, limited temperature resistance (about 80°C dry heat and 60°C wet heat), contains solvents which may be physiologically harmful; not resistant against plant oils, fats, and various solvents (e.g., benzene, trichlorethylene, and carbon tetrachloride).
  *b. Chlorinated rubber–alkyd resin:*  Same as a. Chemical resistance is less than a.

*Uses*
  *a. Chlorinated rubber:*  Paints used in the chemical industry (e.g., metal treatment plants), coke works, dye works, laundries.
  *b. Chlorinated rubber-alkyd resins:*  Paints used for ships, breweries, coke works, and in the chemical industry.
  *c. Chlorinated rubber added to oil paints:*  Paints used in areas exposed to dusty conditions, and when painting has to be completed in a short time, etc.

---

*Type of medium*  Cyclized rubber

*Fundamentals*  There are three basic types:
  a. Cyclized rubber with plasticizer to form a medium.
  b. Cyclized rubber in combination with other media (e.g., alkyd resin).
  c. Cyclized rubber as a minor additive to oil paints.

*Paint properties* Weather, water, and chemical resistant, with similar properties to chlorinated rubber paints. Cyclized rubber paints differ from these mainly by possessing better temperature resistance (with dry heat up to 200°C, with damp heat up to 140 °C).

*Advantages* Because no aromatic hydrocarbons are used as solvents, during application they possess advantages from the point of view of health in comparison to chlorinated rubber paints.

*Disadvantages* Not resistant against various solvents (e.g., gasoline). Poor weather resistance.

*Uses*
  a. *Cyclized rubber:* Paints used in the chemical industry (e.g., metal treatment plants), coke plants, dye works, laundries, breweries, and the water treatment industry.
  b. *Cyclized rubber–alkyd resin:* Paints used for ships, breweries, coke plants, and in the chemical industry.
  c. *Cyclized rubber additives to oil paints:* Paints used in dusty conditions and for rapid paint application, etc.

---

*Type of medium* Polyvinylchloride

*Fundamentals* Heavily chlorinated polyvinylchloride and polyvinylchloride–polyvinylacetate. There are two different basic types:
  a. Polyvinyl resins with plasticizers.
  b. Polyvinyl resins in combination with other media (e.g., alkyd resin).

*Paint properties*
  a. *Polyvinyl resins:* Paints with high mineral oil, fat, chemical, and water resistance; nonflammable; satisfactory weather resistance; relatively high surface hardness; good resistance against animal and plant fats and various solvents.
  b. *Polyvinyl resin–alkyd resin:* Paints where lower demands are made regarding chemical resistance and surface hardness.

*Advantages* Paints capable of being used for very many different purposes, with rapid drying properties.

*Disadvantages* Low dry layer thickness, limited temperature resistance (about 70°C dry and 60°C wet heat) due to the type of solvents used (esters, ketones). Obnoxious vapors are produced during application. Great care must be taken that adequate ventilation is provided in enclosed spaces.

*Uses*
  a. *Polyvinyl resins:* Paints used in the chemical industry, in metal treatment plants, coke plants, dye works, laundries, breweries, and in water treatment plants.
  b. *Polyvinyl resin–alkyd resin:* Paints used for ships, breweries, coke plants and in the chemical industry.

---

## Table 6.16. Properties of Synthetic Paints—Two-Part Coatings. (*Source: Wesche*)

*Type of medium* Polyurethane resins

*Fundamentals* Two-part system, based on materials such as desmophen (polyester as carrier for hydroxyl groups) and desmodur (carrier for isocyanate groups), which react together to form a plastic type of product, which is polyurethane.

*Paint properties* High chemical resistance, particularly against somewhat acid substances, water, solvents, fats, and oils. Reasonable resistance against aromatic and aliphatic hydrocarbons and numerous solvents. Considerable surface smoothness and hardness. Temperature resistance up to about 120°C.

*Advantages* Can be used for numerous different purposes, particularly when high chemical resistance is required.

*Disadvantages* Is more difficult to work in comparison to one-part paints. Has less resistance against heavier alkali exposure. In such cases epoxy resin paint are better.

*Uses* Paints used in the chemical industry for water treatment plants, in ship building (internal treatment of surfaces for tankers), the textile industry, oil refineries, the coke industry, and breweries.

*Type of medium* Epoxy resins.

*Fundamentals* Two-part paints based on epoxy resin, which reacts with added amines, amides or isocyanates, to form a plastic product.

*Paint properties* Good chemical resistance, particularly against alkalis. Good resistance against water, solvents, oils, and mineral oils. Good surface smoothness and hardness. Temperature resistance up to about 120° C.

*Advantages* Can be used for numerous different purposes particularly against various types of chemical exposure.

*Disadvantages* More difficult to apply in comparison to one-part paints. Less resistance against acids. Under acid conditions polyurethane paints are better.

*Uses* Paints used in the chemical industry, the water treatment industry, in ship building (internal coatings of tankers), the textile industry, oil refineries, coke plants, and breweries.

*Type of medium* Unsaturated polyester resins.

*Fundamentals* Solutions of unsaturated polyesters in monomers which are liquid and can be easily polymerized form polymers when a peroxide is added. Polymerization can also take place at low temperatures when an activator of this type is added.

*Paint properties* Good water, solvent, mineral oil, and chemical resistance. Temperature resistance up to about 120° C.

*Advantages* It is possible to apply layer thickness between 600 and 1000 microns by the use of brush or spray gun in two working stages. With polyester coatings there is no appreciable shrinkage by solvent evaporation, as the styrene monomer which acts as solvent is polymerized into the structure and acts as medium.

*Disadvantages* The paint must be applied within one hour. It is highly viscous and therefore rather difficult to apply. It has less resistance than epoxy resins or polyurethane resins. Often a final coating of epoxy resin or polyurethane is applied on top of such polyester coatings.

*Uses* Paints used in the chemical industry, the water treatment industry, in ship building (internal paints used for tankers), the textile industry, in oil refineries, coke plants, and breweries.

*Type of medium* Combinations of two-part paints and bitumen.

*Fundamentals* Bituminous materials with polyurethane and epoxy resin constituents.

*Paint properties* Resistance against chemicals, solvents and heat (about 100° C) is less than with the pure two-part coating materials, but appreciably better than that of other bituminous paints.

*Advantages* Cheaper than pure two-part paints, because it can be applied in thicker layers.

*Disadvantages* Only the colors black and red-brown are available. Resistance against weathering is limited.

*Uses* Paints where color does not matter (e.g., painting under water), steel water tanks, coke plants, the steel industry (blast furnaces), and the chemical industry.

*Type of medium*   Polychloroprene and chlorosulfonated polyethylene
*Fundamentals*   These are marketed under the trade names Neoprene, Perbunan C, and Hypalon. They are usually multicomponent paints, which are made by adding accelerators and vulcanizers to Neoprene and Hypalon solutions.
*Paint properties*   Elastic abrasion, water, mineral oil, and fat resistant paints, which are also quite solvent resistant. Can be used both as paints and as applied layers. The material is a type of rubber which can, however, be applied to surfaces on the building site.
*Advantages*   The layers can be applied in thicknesses of between 1.5 and 3 mm.
*Disadvantages*   High grade sand blasting is necessary as surface pretreatment. 6–12 working processes, difficult to work, limited thermal stability (to about 80°C).
*Uses*   Paints used in the chemical industry, steel industry, ship building, textile industry, mining industry, etc.

*Type of medium*   Silicone resins and butyltitanate.
*Fundamentals*   High temperature resistant paint coatings. Can withstand permanent temperatures of up to 260°C when pigmented with aluminum, zinc powder, etc. The heat stability is about 450°C with butyltitanate and up to 600° with silicone.
*Advantages*   Very good temperature resistance which had not been achieved previously by any other medium.
*Disadvantages*   Rust removal grade 3 is an essential requirement for surface pretreatment.
*Uses*   Heat resistant coatings of sheet steel chimneys, radiators, melting furnaces, corner tube furnaces, exhaust pipes, cracking towers, etc.

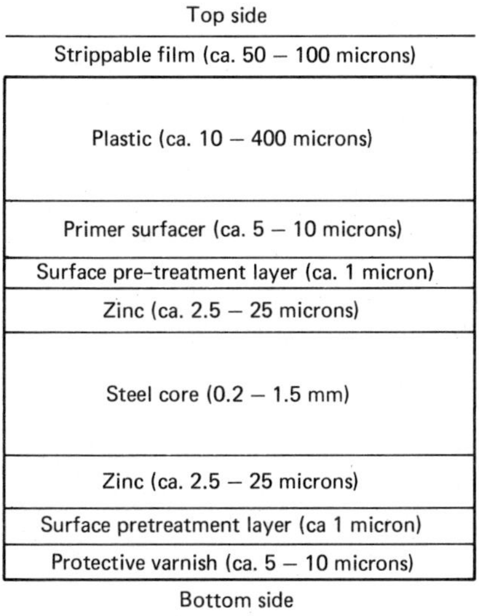

Top side

| Strippable film (ca. 50 – 100 microns) |
| --- |
| Plastic (ca. 10 – 400 microns) |
| Primer surfacer (ca. 5 – 10 microns) |
| Surface pre-treatment layer (ca. 1 micron) |
| Zinc (ca. 2.5 – 25 microns) |
| Steel core (0.2 – 1.5 mm) |
| Zinc (ca. 2.5 – 25 microns) |
| Surface pretreatment layer (ca 1 micron) |
| Protective varnish (ca. 5 – 10 microns) |

Bottom side

**Figure 6.12.** Diagram of layers of hot dipped zinc coated steel sheet, which is covered on one side by a plastic film.

*6.2.3.2.5   Plastic coatings*

A number of materials are protected against corrosion at the factory. These include plastic coated metal sheeting and pipes.

Steel sheeting and galvanized steel sheeting can be covered by the steel manufacturers either on one side only or on both sides with plastics such as polyvinylchloride, PTFE (Teflon and the like), alkyd resin, and acrylic resin. Figure 6.12 shows how these coatings are applied. These steel sheets, which can either be of a single color or multicolored, are used both in the open air (balcony railings, façades etc.) and indoors (partitions, sliding doors, etc).

Pipelines with factory applied coatings are used for long distance transportation of media underground, or for the disposal of effluents. Containers can be supplied ready coated with a plastic covering, either on one side or on both sides. All junctions have to be covered over after installation. Double-face adhesive plastic tapes are used for this purpose; these tapes are wound around the joints with ample overlap.

# 7
# CORROSION AND
# CORROSION PROTECTION
# OF ORGANIC BUILDING
# MATERIALS

## 7.1 TIMBER

Timber corrodes (weathers) in the atmosphere only on the surface by the action of light, moisture and oxygen. It takes on a gray tint. Timber components which are always kept dry or which are kept permanently under water have almost unlimited durability. Alternating frequently between the dry and the wet states reduces the durability considerably. Timber has good resistance against weak acids and alkalis as well as many other chemicals. It is therefore frequently used in places where steel and concrete corrode badly, e.g., in the alkali industry.

The destruction of timber by biological agents, which is strictly speaking not really corrosion at all and is therefore only mentioned briefly, is of much greater importance. Rotting of timber is a biochemical process which takes place when the water content of the timber is in the range of about 20–60%, at temperatures between about +3°C and +40°C (37–104°F), in stagnant air and relatively dark conditions. The action of fungi such as dry rot, wet rot, brown rot, cellar rot, etc. decomposes cellulose and hemicellulose.

Insects can also destroy timber. With dry timber the main danger is from ambrosia beetles, longhorn beetles, powder post beetles, furniture beetles, death watch beetles, and termites. In marine conditions the main dangers are from gribbles, molluscs, and teredos or ship worms.

Apart from taking suitable precautions during building, such as the removal of the bark from timber, good ventilation; and preventing access of moisture, there are several effective chemical measures which can be taken. Timber protecting fluids penetrate the wood and are poisonous to fungi and insects (fungicides and insecticides). Oily materials such as a mixture of phenol and coal tar, as well as chloronaphthalene, and water soluble salts such as example $MgSiF_6$, $KF \cdot HF$, $Na_3AsO_3$, are used. Further details can be obtained from specialized literature dealing with timber protection.

## 7.2 BITUMINOUS BUILDING MATERIALS

The thermoplastic building materials bitumen and asphalt are virtually insoluble in water. Because of their extremely densely packed hydrocarbon molecules they are practically impervious to water. They have good resistance against acids and alkalis as well as against salt solutions. With rising temperature and concentration of the corroding medium the rate of attack increases, but increasing the hardness of the bituminous building materials makes them more resistant.

Bitumen is dissolved by other petroleum fractions such as gasoline and oil, but coal tar pitch is not similarly soluble. Chlorinated hydrocarbons such as carbon tetrachloride and trichlorethylene, as well as carbon disulfide, dissolve both bitumen and pitch.

Bitumen only oxidizes in air very slowly. In contrast, oxygen and light act on pitch and cause it to age. This is the reason for its tendency to harden and to become more brittle when exposed to the weather. This progress of ageing is more rapid than would be predicted in terms of the loss of volatile materials. It is suspected that the oxidation of unsaturated hydrocarbons results in the production of resinlike molecules. In the ground and under water the ageing process is appreciably slower. As ageing continues adhesion is reduced. Pitch has particularly good wetting and capillary penetration properties.

Bitumen has no effect on living organisms but coal tar pitch is antibiotic (fungicide and bactericide), and the roots of plants are unable to penetrate it. Various types of bituminous building materials are available, and are employed as cements in road building and as cements and water barriers when building in groundwater. They are also used for roofing felts, as adhesives and water barriers for sealing gaps, in pipeline construction for jointing and sealing, and as adhesives for flooring and floor coverings. There is no need to make special provisions for corrosion protection, because bituminous materials are used as corrosion protection and building protection media in their own right. If coal tar pitch and bitumen paints are combined, however, there is a danger that oily layers may be formed which impair adhesion.

Protective paints for application on metallic and non-metallic building surfaces are produced both from coal tar pitch and from varying grades of petroleum bitumen (high vacuum bitumen, distilled bitumen, blown bitumen, etc.). The surface should usually be pretreated as for other paints (see section 6.2.3.2.2). Minimum layer thicknesses of 200–400 microns are required, depending on corrosive conditions. Combinations of coal tar pitch and epoxy resin, or coal tar pitch filled with asbestos, provide particularly durable films.

Bitumen and coal tar pitch are used for more or less the same ranges and types of use, but in each case it is necessary to consider their special properties (e.g., antibiotic action, ageing and wetting properties). For example, for drinking water supply only bitumen paints can be used; paint films made from coal tar pitch are usually better for corrosion protection of steel parts under water.

## 7.3 PLASTICS

### 7.3.1 Plastics as Building Materials

Plastics, which are highly polymerized organic materials, usually consist of a dense, resinous substance. Plastics have good corrosion resistance; this depends however, on composition, buildup, and manner of use. Most plastics are not attacked by water or aqueous solutions (acids, alkalis, salt solutions) and many plastics are also resistant to solvents and fuels. Tables 7.1 and 7.2 show the behavior of important plastics against aggressive media. Damage by biological agents is found particularly in hot and damp climates. (e.g. algae, termites)

It is not usual to protect plastic surfaces. Plastics are affected much more severely than other building materials by various environmental conditions over periods of time (i.e., they age). The ageing process is influenced by the weather: variations of ambient temperature; moisture in the air in the form of fog, rain, snow, hail, and water vapor; air impurities; ultra-violet radiation; wind; etc. Physical factors, (e.g., mechanical stresses, static electricity) and chemical agents (e.g., salt solutions; oxygen) have some influence; the combined action of these variables causes such chemical reactions as oxidation, displacement, and double displacement reactions. Absorption of water, evaporation, swelling, precipitation, and other factors all take part in this process, which breaks up the macromolecules, thus causing a change in properties. Chemical resistance, surface structure, color and gloss are all affected, and embrittlement can take place. The ageing process can be slowed down by careful manufacture and use of special additives.The additives should stabilize the molecular structure, filter out ultraviolet light and longer wave radiation, and reduce oxidation tendencies; such materials are called stabilizers, light filters, and antioxidants, respectively. The weather resistance of plastics as well as their degree of ageing vary very considerably. Good weather resistance is shown by polytetrafluorethylene (Teflon etc.) and phenolic and amino plastics; polyamides, polystyrene, polyethylene, and polyvinylchloride are not as good in this respect.

The ageing reactions are so complicated that they are not as yet fully known. It is not possible to forecast exactly how fast ageing is likely to proceed under given conditions.

### 7.3.2  Plastics in Corrosion Protection

Plastics are used for corrosion protection in the form of paints, coatings, etc. Tables 7.1 and 7.2 describe the stability of plastic protective coatings against various aggressive media. Some examples follow.

Chlorinated rubber and epoxy resins with polyamide hardener are used for the protection of zinc coated parts. Polyethylene adhesive tapes are employed for winding around pipelines which are to be buried in soil. Acid-proof coatings and claddings are made from polyvinylchloride. Polytetrafluorethylene shows particularly good resistance against aggressive media and can be used, for example, for the cladding of containers and for coating sheet steel. Polyurethane lacquer is used for weather and chemical proof coatings on aluminum.

**Table 7.1.   Standard Values of the Chemical Resistance and Water Absorption of Important Plastics**

| | Acids | | | Alkalis | | Solvents | | | | | Fuels | | | Oils | | | Water Absorption |
|---|---|---|---|---|---|---|---|---|---|---|---|---|---|---|---|---|---|
| | weak | strong | oxidizing | weak | strong | alcohols | esters | ketones | ethers | alkyl halides | benzene | gasoline | mixture of fuels | mineral oil | animal and plant | oils and fats | |
| Polyvinyl chloride (PVC) hard | + | + | ⊕ | + | + | + | − | − | − | ⊘ | − | + | ⊘ | + | + | + | 3...20 |
| soft | + | ⊕ | ○ | + | ○ | ⊕ | − | − | − | − | − | ⊕ | − | ○ | ○ | ○ | ≈20 |
| Polyethylene (PE) hard | + | + | − | + | + | + | + | + | ○ | ⊘ | ○ | ⊕ | ⊕ | ⊕ | + | + | ≈0 |
| soft | + | + | − | + | + | ○ | ○ | ○ | ○ | − | − | ⊘ | − | ○ | ⊕ | ⊘ | ≈0 |
| Polypropylene (PP) | + | + | − | + | + | + | ⊕ | ⊕ | ○ | ⊘ | ⊘ | ⊘ | ○ | ○ | + | + | ≈0 |
| Polyisobutylene (PIB) | + | + | ○ | + | + | + | − | ⊖ | − | − | − | − | − | − | + | + | ≈0 |
| Polystyrene (PS) | + | ⊕ | ○ | + | + | + | − | − | − | − | − | ○ | − | ○ | + | + | ≈0 |
| Polymethyl methacrylate (PMMA) | + | + | ○ | + | + | ○ | − | − | ○ | − | − | + | + | + | + | + | 45 |
| Phenolic resins | + | − | − | − | + | + | + | + | + | + | + | + | + | + | + | + | <20 |
| Aminoresins (melamine formaldehyde, urea formaldehyde) | ○ | − | ⊕ | − | − | + | + | + | + | + | + | + | + | + | + | + | 200...400 |
| Polyester resins (UP) | + | + | − | ○ | ⊖ | ⊕ | ⊕ | − | − | − | ⊕ | + | + | + | + | + | ≈20 |
| Polyamides (PA) | − | − | − | + | ○ | + | + | + | + | + | + | + | ⊕ | + | + | + | 100...1000 |
| Polyurethane (PUR) | + | ⊘ | + | + | ○ | + | + | ⊘ | + | ⊘ | + | + | + | + | + | + | <100 |
| Polytetrafluoroethylene (PTFE) | + | + | + | + | ⊕ | + | ○ | ⊕ | + | + | + | + | + | + | + | + | ≈0 |
| Epoxy resins (EP) | + | + | − | + | + | + | ○ | ⊘ | + | ○ | ⊘ | + | + | + | + | + | <10 |
| Polycarbonate (PC) | + | + | ○ | + | − | ⊘ | ○ | ○ | − | − | ○ | + | + | + | + | + | ≈10 |

Symbols:  + resistant, ⊕ fairly resistant, ○ resistant under certain circumstances, ⊖ mainly nonresistant, − totally nonresistant

**Table 7.2.   Standard Values of the Chemical Resistance of Important Elastomers.**

| Elastomer | Oxidation | Mineral oil | Organic Solvents | Water, Acids, Alkalis |
|-----------|-----------|-------------|------------------|------------------------|
| Natural rubber | ○ | ⊖ | − | ⊕ |
| Chlorinated rubber | + | + | − | + |
| Polysulfide rubber | + | + | + | ⊕ |
| Silicone rubber | + | + | + | ⊖ |
| Polyurethane rubber | + | + | + | |

Symbols:   +  resistant,  ⊕  fairly resistant
           ○  resistant under certain circumstances
           ⊖  mainly nonresistant
           −  totally nonresistant

Specific uses of plastics for corrosion protection of building materials are commonly specified in connection with the appropriate building material.

# 8
# CHEMICAL TESTS OF CORROSIVE MEDIA

The simple tests given here can be carried out by the nonchemist outside a chemical laboratory. These tests give important information but naturally cannot and should not replace laboratory tests; the tests described here should mainly be used as aids in the examination of the media which are in contact with building materials (mostly aqueous solutions), to indicate the likely presence of aggressive materials. If there is the slightest suspicion that corrosion could occur some time in the future it is necessary to consult an experienced chemical laboratory, which can carry out more exact tests.

It is absolutely essential to use correct sampling techniques. When samples are taken, and during storage, before testing, no substances must be allowed to escape (e.g., carbon dioxide, water by evaporation) or be added (dilution by rainwater). As far as possible, samples should be taken at different times. Impure waters should usually be filtered before examination.

To assess the likelihood of attack on concrete it is particularly important to determine the sulfate, carbon dioxide, ammonium, and magnesium contents of the surrounding medium as well as the total hardness, chlorides, sulfides and $p$H. Indicator papers and solutions and other simpler methods are available for all these tests. Semi-quantitative results can be obtained by dipping indicator paper in or adding indicator solution to the sample to be investigated, and then comparing it with the color scales supplied.

If attack on metals is to be expected, it is particularly important to determine chloride, sulfate, sulfide, nitrate, and ammonium concentrations and $pH$. Simple indicator methods can also be used for these tests.

The measurement of $pH$ is an example of such a method. A strip of universal indicator paper ($pH$ 1–13) is dipped into the water sample. The color of the indicator paper is then compared with the appropriate color scale and the result is read off in whole $pH$ units (Figure 8.1). To obtain a more exact figure special indicator paper is chosen depending

**Figure 8.1.** Determination of pH by means of universal indicator sticks.

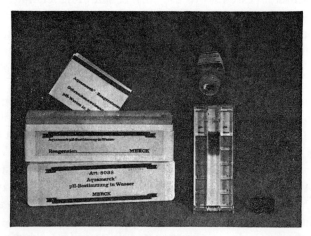

**Figure 8.2.** Determination of pH with indicator liquid in a vessel with three chambers.

upon the $pH$ range obtained (e.g., $pH$ 5.5–9 or 9–13). When this is dipped into a new sample of the water, the $pH$ can be found with an accuracy of at least one-half a $pH$ unit.

Nonbleeding indicator rods are particularly useful. These are indicator papers set into plastic. The indicator dyes are bound to cellulose fibers in such a way that they cannot be washed out. If such a rod becomes dirty, the impurities can be carefully washed off with distilled water. Both universal and special indicator rods are obtainable. These small indicator rods must remain in the water until no further change in color can be observed. With unbuffered waters this can take 10 minutes or longer.

It is possible to determine the $pH$ immediately, using a liquid indicator mix (test solution) with its test vessel and color scale, provided the water is clear and colorless. A certain quantity of indicator is added dropwise to the measured water sample and the color obtained is compared with the color scale. This consists of a series of colored liquids sealed into glass tubes (Figures 8.2). The accuracy is ±0.5 $pH$ units. The $pH$ can be determined more accurately in the laboratory by means of a potentiometer (±0.1 $pH$ units).

# LITERATURE AND SUGGESTED READING

Virtually all the literature references given in the original text are in the German language. Much reference is made to the various DIN specifications (Deutsche Industrielle Normen), which are the standard West German industrial specifications equivalent to the British BSS and the American ASTM specifications. The DIN specifications can be purchased from any German bookseller and from many of the larger city booksellers in the United States as well.

Most American readers are, however, more interested in further reading references in the English language. For this reason the translator suggests the following titles.

*Chapter 2*

T. D. Larsson, *Portland Cement and Asphalt Concretes.* McGraw-Hill, New York, 1963.

H. F. Taylor, *The Chemistry of Cements.* 2 vols. Academic Press, New York, 1964.

R. S. Boynton, *Chemistry and Technology of Lime and Limestone.* Interscience Publishers, New York, 1966.

G. E. Troxell, H. E. Davis, and J. W. Kelly, *Composition and Properties of Concrete.* 2nd edition. McGraw-Hill, New York, 1968.

F. M. Lea, *The Chemistry of Cement and Concrete.* Edwards Arnold, London, 1970.

*Chapter 3*

F. H. Clews, *Heavy Clay Technology.* British Ceramic Society, London, 1955.

W. W. Kriegel and H. Palmour, *Mechanical Properties of Engineering Ceramics.* Interscience, New York, 1961.
G. H. Stewart, *Science of Ceramics.* 3 volumes. Academic Press, New York, 1967.
J. W. Simpson, *The Weathering and Performance of Building Materials.* Horrobin, London, 1970.

*Chapter 4*

W. A Weyl and E. C. Marboe, *The Constitution of Glasses.* 2 vols. Interscience, New York, 1964.
L. Holland, *The Properties of Glass Surfaces.* Chapman and Hall, London, 1964.

*Chapter 5*

F. N. Hatch et al., *Petrology of the Igneous Rocks.* Murby, London, 1972.
H. Blatt et al., *Origin of Sedimentary Rocks.* Prentice-Hall, Englewood Cliffs, New Jersey, 1972.
A. Short and W. Kinniburgh, *Lightweight Concrete.* CR Books, London, 1963.
*Minerals Yearbook.* US Department of the Interior, Bureau of Mines, 1973.
*Also some of the books mentioned under chapter 2.*

*Chapter 6*

U. R. Evans, *The Corrosion and Oxidation of Metals.* Edward Arnold, London, 1960.
E. Rabald, *Corrosion Guide.* Elsevier, Amsterdam, 1968.
G. Butler and H. C. K. Ison, *Corrosion and its Prevention in Waters.* L. Hill, London, 1966.
H. Uhlig, *Corrosion and Corrosion Control.* John Wiley, New York, 1971.
A. Walters and E. H. Hueck van der Plas, *Biodeterioration of Materials.* Applied Science, London, 1971.
W. H. Ailor, *Handbook on Corrosion.* John Wiley & Sons, New York, 1971.
J. F. Scully, *The Fundamentals of Corrosion.* Pergamon, Oxford, 1975.

A. D. Mercer and C. J. L. Booker, *Corrosion of Metals and Alloys.* NLL, Boston Spa, Lincs., England, 1967.

P. Nylen and E. Sunderland, *Modern Surface Coatings.* Interscience, New York, 1965.

W. von Fischer, *Paint and Varnish Technology.* Hafner, New York, 1964.

D. H. Parker, *Principles of Surface Coating Technology.* 2 vols. Interscience, New York, 1965.

*Chapter 7*

W. P. K. Findley, *The Preservation of Timber.* Black, London, 1962.

A. J. Panshin, *Textbook of Wood Technology.* McGraw-Hill, New York, 1964.

A. E. Hoiberg, *Bituminous Materials.* 3 vols. Interscience, New York, 1964–1966.

H. Abraham, *Asphalts and Allied Substances.* 5 vols. Van Nostrand, New York, 1960–1963.

L. Bateman, *The Chemistry and Physics of Rubberlike Substances.* MacLaren, London, 1963.

I. Skeist, *Plastics in Building.* Reinhold, New York, 1966.

T. C. Patton, *Alkyd Resin Technology.* Interscience, New York, 1962.

W. S. Penn, *PVC Technology.* MacLaren, London, 1966.

J. Bjorkstem, *Polyesters and Their Applications.* Reinhold, New York, 1956.

H. Du Bois and F. W. John, *Plastics.* Reinhold, New York, 1967.

Reference should be made to the various trade associations the addresses of which appear in the yellow pages of your local telephone directory.

Finally the translator would like to mention his own two books in the field which are:

R. M. E. Diamant, *The Chemistry of Building Materials.* Business Books, London, 1970.

R. M. E. Diamant, *The Prevention of Corrosion.* Business Books, London, 1971.

# INDEX

# INDEX